HORRIBLE SCIENCE

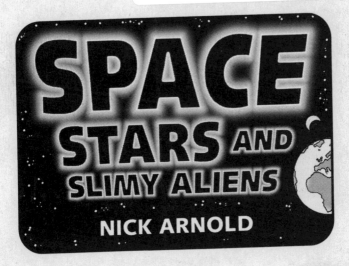

SPACE
STARS AND
SLIMY ALIENS

NICK ARNOLD

Illustrated by
Tony De Saulles

Hippo

Scholastic Children's Books,
Commonwealth House, 1-19 New Oxford Street,
London WC1A 1NU, UK

A division of Scholastic Ltd
London ~ New York ~ Toronto ~ Sydney ~ Auckland
Mexico City ~ New Delhi ~ Hong Kong

First published in the UK by Scholastic Ltd, 2003

Text copyright © Nick Arnold, 2003
Illustrations copyright © Tony De Saulles, 2003

ISBN 0 439 97866 1

Typeset by Falcon Oast Graphic Art Ltd, East Hoathly, Sussex
Printed and bound by Nørhaven Paperback A/S, Denmark

2 4 6 8 10 9 7 5 3 1

The right of Nick Arnold and Tony De Saulles to be identified as the author and
illustrator of this work respectively has been asserted by them in accordance
with the Copyright, Designs and Patents Act, 1988.

Contents

WHO'S LEFT THIS REVOLTING, SMELLY SLIME TRAIL? READ ON TO FIND OUT...

Nick Arnold has been writing stories and books since he was a youngster, but never dreamt he'd find fame writing about outer space. His research involved staring at stars, being turned down for astronaut training and trying to burp in space – and he enjoyed every minute of it.

When he's not delving into Horrible Science, he spends his spare time eating pizza, riding his bike and thinking up corny jokes (though not all at the same time).

Tony De Saulles picked up his crayons when he was still in nappies and has been doodling ever since. He takes Horrible Science very seriously and even agreed to jump into a black hole. Fortunately, he has made a full recovery.

When he's not out with his sketchpad, Tony likes to write poetry and play squash, though he hasn't written any poetry about squash yet.

INTRODUCTION

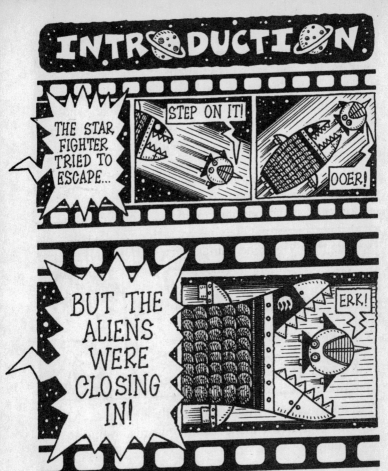

Space movies are great, aren't they? Don't you just love the speeding spacecraft, perishing planets and slimy slobbering aliens. And isn't it a pity when some tedious teacher says, "Oh, but it's all made-up"? But what they don't tell you is that real-life outer space is even more scary than the scariest space movie!

In a moment, we'll blast into space to boldly go where no science book has gone before. Our mission is to find out why space is so scary. And why just going for a walk in space without your spacesuit can make your guts explode and your eyeballs plop out of your head.

Then, if we survive outer space, we'll be peering at putrid planets and sizzling stars and mad moons. Horrible places, the lot of them. And we'll be finding out fearsome, foul and funny facts such as…

• How the Sun *sings*.
• Why you can't burp in space.
• Which stars turn you into slime.
• And why your body bits are made of blown-up stars.

Yes, these and many more facts really are true … er, hold on … our space expert, Luke Upwards, wants to say something…

Oh all right! Scientists aren't sure if aliens exist. And if you must know, I made up the alien story in this book.

Mind you – we will be looking at our chances of meeting real-life aliens.

But the rest is really real – even if it sounds like it's off on another planet. And hopefully you'll feel that space is an out-of-this-world subject and you'll be encouraged to find out more. And who knows? Maybe one day you'll become an astronaut and live your own true-life space adventures.

So who needs movies? Just grab your popcorn and settle down in your seat. The show is about to begin!

SPLATTERING SPACE

Earth is a small blue ball floating in a big black sea. And the big black sea is as dark and dangerous as a bad-tempered black bear in a coal cellar! Later on we'll find out how deadly dangerous space really is – but first it's time to check out the basic background bits.

So what's floating about up there?

Slimy space fact file

NAME: Stuff in space

THE BASIC FACTS: Here are the main things that you might see in space...

COOL!

Stars – giant balls of super-hot gases. (Our Sun is actually a star.) Even the smallest stars are 80 times bigger than the biggest planets. (To find out more, see page 21.)

Galaxies – swirling whirls of billions of stars.

ASTRONOMICAL!

WHAT ON EARTH IS THAT?

Planets – big balls of rock or gas that orbit (go round) a star. The time a planet takes to make one orbit of its star is called a year. Planets spin in space and one whole turn is called a day.

Solar System – the Sun and the planets that orbit it.

Moons – rocky objects that orbit planets.

BY JUPITER!

Asteroids – large space rocks that orbit the Sun. Most of them hang out in an area called the Asteroid Belt. (The details are on page 91.)

ROCK ON!

COMET

Comets – balls of ice and rock that orbit the Sun on the edge of the Solar System. Some comets fly close to the Sun. (For more details, why not steer your spacecraft to page 128.)

SLIMY SECRETS: Some stars aren't lucky stars if you go too near them. These twinkling terrors could cook you to a puddle of slime. (If you're interested and feeling really brave you can turn to pages 26–29 for the dangerous details.)

THIS "STAR TREATMENT" ISN'T ALL IT'S CRACKED UP TO BE...

Wouldn't it be great to think that all these stars were really close and we could get to them in about five minutes. But they're not – they're all fantastically far away. To find out quite how big space is, why not try this experiment.

Take a grain of sand (younger readers could use their teacher's brain, a stick insect's eyeball or pocket money – so long as it's pitifully small). Balance the sand on your fingertip and stretch out your arm. Hold your fingertip up against the sky. Can you still see the grain of sand? Great! Your eyesight's better than mine!

Now, imagine that your incredible eyeballs are as powerful as space telescopes and that you're staring at a squitty speck of sky the size of that grain of sand. How many stars would you see?

Here are three possibilities…

a) Not a sausage. The sky is emptier than a piggy bank after a Christmas shopping trip.

b) Two stars.

c) 200,000 billion stars.

Answer:
c) There really are 200,000 billion stars in every grain-of-sand-sized bit of sky.

And now for a quick time-out to do with BIG numbers

There are a lot of big numbers in this book. Here's an idea of how big is BIG. In 2002, champion laundry man

Chick Shung Chui retired after ironing *one million* shirts. So that's one million – and it had taken him 53 years ironing at a speed of 36 shirts an hour. But to iron one billion shirts, Mr Chick would have had to work for 53 THOUSAND years. And I hope there's less ironing to do in your house.

In a moment, I'll tell you some things that almost made my head explode, but first let's check out the Hubble Space Telescope. This powerful telescope has been orbiting the Earth since 1990. And it really has peered at a tiny speck of sky and seen 200,000 billion stars. I bet the papers gave loads of space to the story (loads of *space* – geddit?!)…

THE DAILY SOLAR SYSTEM
15 January 1996

WOTTA LOTTA SPACE!

Scientists are stunned by the latest findings from the Hubble Space Telescope.

Even in a tiny bit of sky there are 2,000 galaxies. Earth-based telescopes can see billions of stars, but clouds and dusty air can spoil the view. The Hubble telescope has a much clearer view from outside the Earth's atmosphere. Said one awe-struck astronomer, "It makes me feel very small and spaced-out!" She then disappeared into a darkened room with a cup of tea and a headache pill.

But actually the paper missed the really BIG story. It's so mind-mashingly MASSIVE that my brain nearly blew up when I heard it…

ERK!

WARNING! YOU'D BEST PUT ON A CRASH HELMET BEFORE READING THIS NEXT BIT!

The BIG story (hang on to that crash helmet!)

That speck of sky was *nothing special*. If you pointed the Hubble telescope at millions of other specks of sky you'd see just as many stars. And that means … help, where's my calculator?! There could be 40 BILLION GALAXIES – that's 4,000 BILLION BILLION STARS in the sky. Many of these stars might have planets whizzing around them – including worlds like our Earth! In all, scientists reckon there could be ONE BILLION planets like Earth in our galaxy! But hang on, there's EVEN MORE…

This is just what the Hubble Space Telescope can see – but there may well be billions of more-distant stars that it can't make out. As it is, some of the starlight picked up by the Hubble Telescope had been zipping our way at 300,000 km a second for more than ten billion years. I guess it must be "travelling light" ha ha! Anyway, that's enough brain-busting bits for now. Er, I hope your brain isn't steaming too much!

Over to us

But before I go on, I really ought to mention where we fit into all this. Aha – that's us here…

You're looking at our very own galaxy – the Milky Way. You can actually see the Milky Way if you happen to live somewhere that's really dark at night – like a place in the country, far away from street lights. It looks like a huge milky drool dribbled across the night sky by a giant baby...

Except it's not milk. It's stars. Something like 200,000 billion stars, in fact. And they're bunched together because you're gazing at them from the side (imagine looking at a dish from the side and you'll get the idea...)

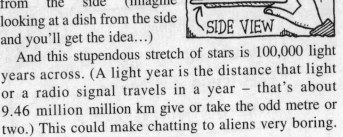

And this stupendous stretch of stars is 100,000 light years across. (A light year is the distance that light or a radio signal travels in a year – that's about 9.46 million million km give or take the odd metre or two.) This could make chatting to aliens very boring.

13

I mean, a brief phone chat with some slimy aliens from our own galaxy could take *ten thousand* years. Your phone bills would be ASTRONOMICAL!

HAVE YOU KIDS BEEN PHONING ALIENS?

But although it's incredibly big, the Milky Way is just part of a group of over 40 galaxies called the Local Group (it might be local but it's still billions of kilometres across). And the Local Group is just one of 400 groups of galaxies that are together known as the Local Supercluster. So for any aliens reading this, here's our full postal address…

Earth
The Solar System
Orion arm
(that's one of the swirling sticking out bits)
The Milky Way
The Local Group
The Local Supercluster
The Universe
OOPS Sorry I've forgotten the postcode.

Dear Earthlings
Found you at last! Must pop round for tea sometime!
Love the Aliens XXX

Mind you, space is so horribly huge, it might take a few million years for that postcard to arrive.

OK, so space is seriously sizeable, but here's the most spine-tingling space statistic of all. It's not how BIG space is, it's how *empty* it is! Scientists say that space is 99.9999% nothing – that's zero, zilch, diddly squat. Space is nearly all empty … er, space! In other words, if the universe was a huge room 30 km wide and 30 km high, all the stars and galaxies and planets and slime ice cream from the Planet Splott would scrunch up into an itsy-bitsy grain of sand.

But isn't that where we started?!

Well, now you've found out a bit about space, I bet you can't wait to leap into your spacesuit and go and see space for yourself!

Not so fast! You don't think you'd be allowed to whizz off in a multi-billion dollar spacecraft just like that, do you?

You need *years* of training before you're allowed near one of those things. But while you're waiting for your training to start, you can always read our super sci-fi space story. And guess what? The first episode shows what space is *really* like…

Oddblob's Alien Adventure

GREETINGS. MY NAME'S ODDBLOB FROM THE PLANET BLURB... I USED TO BE A SPACE EXPLORER, BUT NOW I'M IN THE INTERGALACTIC ADVENTURE HOLIDAY BUSINESS. HERE'S MY BROCHURE...

≥ Get away from it all with ≤
ODDBLOB'S ADVENTURE TOURS

Relax in our luxury chauffeur-driven spacecraft on a guided tour of the SOLAR SYSTEM!

- Brilliant brainy guide (with two brains) – that's me – Oddblob.
- Action, adventure and fun for all the family!
- All types of alien welcome, just so long as you pay and don't eat each other!
- NINE planets, one Sun and lots of moons to explore!
- Stunning, super space walks (spacesuits provided).

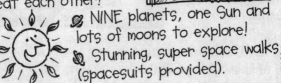

"These tours are the best holidays in the galaxy!" Oddblob the Blurb (no relation)

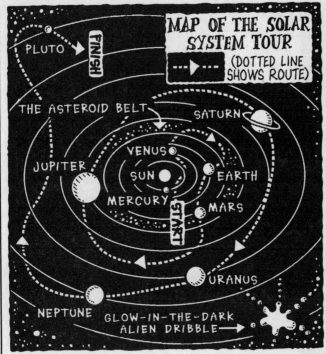

MAP OF THE SOLAR SYSTEM TOUR

---▷--- (DOTTED LINE SHOWS ROUTE)

PLUTO →FINISH

THE ASTEROID BELT

SATURN

JUPITER

VENUS

SUN

EARTH

MERCURY

START

MARS

URANUS

NEPTUNE   GLOW-IN-THE-DARK ALIEN DRIBBLE →

The small print

1. Oddblob will warn you about the dangers of each planet you visit. So you mustn't blame him if you get killed.

2. If you leave the spacecraft, you must remember to put on a spacesuit. If you forget you'll spend your final seconds wishing you had a better memory.

IMPORTANT SCIENCE NOTE

Hmm – sounds like Oddblob's spacecraft is faster than anything known on Earth. Our human spacecraft would take years to travel between the planets. For example, the unmanned Voyager 2 craft was launched in 1977 and didn't get to Neptune until 1989 – that's 12 years later!

My story begins when I took a booking from a family of aliens. They wanted to tour the Solar System, but they were a bit messy… They even left alien dribble on my brochure.

Here's the alien family. Slobslime is a Snotty from the Planet Splott. And she's not the smartest alien in the universe.

HAS ANYONE SEEN MY BRAIN?

GOO GOO — ME SAY HELLO!

And here's her baby, Sloppy. She lives in an egg-pod, but in 100 years time she'll hatch into an adult Snotty like Slobslime.

On the first day of the aliens' holiday I tried to get them used to living in space.

Things went wrong from the start. Our first outing was a walk in space, but Slobslime had forgotten some vital equipment…

ARE WE READY?

YOU BET! I COULD DO WITH SOME FRESH AIR!

YOU'VE FORGOTTEN YOUR SPACESUIT!

Seconds later, Slobslime suffered the effects of being in space without a spacesuit.

Space can be colder than −100°C. That's cold enough to freeze skin solid. Sunlight can be hotter than 120°C, hot enough to burn the skin to a crisp. Slobslime was frozen like a slime-lolly on one side and roasted to a slime-crisp on the other.

With no air to press on Slobslime's body from the outside, the air in her body pushed outwards. Soon her guts, lungs and eyeballs were about to go pop. Without air pressure all her blood and body juices began to boil like slimy green soup.

Deadly rays, known as radiation (ray-de-ay-shun), from the Sun blasted Slobslime. Soon she'd be cooked from the inside like a blurbi-turkey in a microwave With seconds to spare I pulled Slobslime to safety and, after a few hours of body repairs in my spacecraft's sick bay, she was back to her old slimy self.

ANOTHER IMPORTANT SCIENCE NOTE
It looks like Snotties have incredible powers of healing and recovery. Any human who did this would certainly be killed!

So you see, there are a loads of dangers in space – but at least the stars look great. As the Hubble Space Telescope showed, you get a lovely clear view. But you don't have to go into space to see stars… Instead, you could bang your head (though that's not a good idea!).

Or you could point your telescope at the next chapter.

STAGGERING STARS

It's easy to stare at the stars but it's not so easy to explain them. You might even come up with some curious questions…

> HOW ARE STARS MADE?

> HOW DO STARS WORK?

> ARE THEY ALL THE SAME?

OK, OK – here are some answers. Let's start at the beginning (it's better than starting at the end). How are stars made? To find out, I've arranged an exclusive interview with our local friendly star – the Sun…

Megastar Magazine

In this week's issue:

STAR CONFESSIONS

SPOT THE STAR!

THE SUN'S SECRET STORY

21

THE SUN'S SECRET STORY

by our reporter Randall Scandal

He's definitely the biggest star in our Solar System – a legend in his own lifetime. When I met the Sun, he was in a sunny mood in his exclusive home in the centre of the Solar System. For a big 4.6-billion-year-old ball of hydrogen gas, he didn't look at all bad.

Randall: How did you become such a big star?

Sun: I remember it like it was yesterday. Though it wasn't yesterday – it was 4.6 billion years ago.

Randall: So how did it all begin?

Sun: At the time I was nothing. Just a big cloud of dust and gas floating around in space. I was a bit of a drifter.

Randall: But you pulled yourself together?

Sun: You bet I did! I'm not too sure what happened but I figure a passing star gave me a nudge. That's when I started pulling gas and dust into a kind of ball. Those were HAPPY days – I was having a ball! And that's how I got my act together until I landed a STARRING role!

22

Randall: So what happened?

Sun: As I got bigger, I got hotter – that's when I really shone!

Randall: So what was the secret of your success as a star? What really makes you tick?

Sun: Well, I guess if you're a star, you must have what it takes…

Randall: What's that?

Sun: Enough gravity to crush your hydrogen gas into a substance called helium. Star quality – that's what I call it!

Randall: And that gives you energy?

Sun: Some of the hydrogen gets turned into heat and light energy. It certainly keeps me going!

Randall: But in the early days, success didn't come easy – it took a few million years before you became a star.

Sun: Yeah, it was hard work!

Randall: And meanwhile your planets were forming…

Sun: Yeah – that was the outer part of my cloud. They're part of my dazzling success.

Randall: I know, I've got sunburn.

Well, the Sun's got a good memory! The Earth and the other planets really did start off as bits of dust and gas. The bits pulled together to form small rocks. And the small rocks clumped into bigger rocks and then mini-planets. The mini-planets smashed together and the bits joined up to form the planets as they are today.

Now for the question that I bet you're asking at this very second. What was doing all this pulling and smashing of dust and gas and rocks to make stars and solar systems? Without it, we wouldn't be here, so I guess it's a matter of some gravity. Hey, that's the answer – it's a force called gravity!

Greedy, grasping gravity

Gravity is vital for getting a handle on space and everything in it and you've got to know about it to make sense of the rest of this book. But it's a bit *scientific*.

ARGH! NOT AGAIN!

WARNING – SCIENCE FACTS COMING UP!

Slimy space fact file

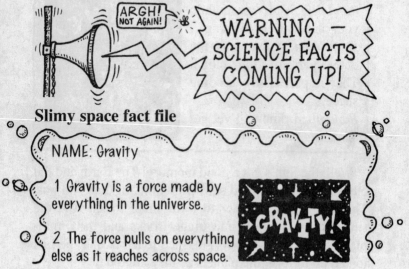

NAME: Gravity

1 Gravity is a force made by everything in the universe.

2 The force pulls on everything else as it reaches across space.

GRAVITY!

3 The Earth's gravity pulls you towards it and your gravity pulls the Earth towards YOU!

YOUR GRAVITY ↑ EARTH'S GRAVITY ↓

4 The further you go from Earth the weaker its pull becomes. But gravity still works billions of kilometres away. That's why the Sun's gravity stops the planets zooming off into space.

SLIMY SECRETS: The bigger and heavier you are, the stronger your gravity is. That's why the Earth (being bigger than you) pulls you down towards it when you jump. Possibly with painful results...

IT'S CRUNCH TIME!

OK, so that's the nitty-gritty of gravity. In a moment, you'll get the chance to see stars with your very own eyes. But first I've got some nasty news about big stars, roughly about ten times the size of the Sun. These heavyweights have horrible habits...

Sinister super-stars' secrets

Big stars are bad news. Would you believe it – before they're even *born* these murderous mega-stars in the making are already causing chaos in the cosmos! Stars of all sizes form in huge clouds of dust and gas (as in the Sun's story on page 22). But as a big star takes shape, it zaps smaller wannabe stars with gas and blasts them to bits.

Big stars are greedy gas guzzlers too. They make more heat and crush hydrogen into helium faster than smaller stars like the Sun. And, after 11 million years, the star crashes inwards – pulled by the force of its own gravity!

The centre bounces out again ... only to hit the outer part of the star which is still falling in!

The BIG BASH bursts the star to bits in a blast brighter than ONE HUNDRED BILLION stars! It's called a supernova and it's a real super-star show-stopper. And that, you might think, is that… After all, the sinister super-star is blown to itsy-witsy bits. Or is it?

You know those horror films where the monster is supposed to be dead but suddenly comes back to life? Well, it happens in real life with big stars…

After the blast, the centre of a star carries on shrinking. But it doesn't die – it turns into a scary mini-monster. It's known as a neutron star.

It's just 20 km across. And you might think that's too small to be dangerous. But here's what happens if you get too close to it…

The neutron star is incredibly heavy. This gives it GIGANTIC gravity. If you landed on a neutron star, the gravity would make your body so heavy that a tiny flake of dried snot would weigh ONE MILLION TONNES. This could make a very large hole in your hankie.

Would you fancy a neutron-star holiday?

Horrible Holidays present...
The Neutron Star Hotel

Check into our out-of-this-world ONE-STAR hotel...

WELCOME!

GASP!

Unique atmosphere! It's so heavy that it's only 2.5 cm high. At least you can enjoy an all-day lie-in as you struggle to breathe!

Work-out in our exclusive gym. Just lifting your head uses more energy than climbing Mount Everest.

URRRRRGH!

You'll want to come back as soon as possible. And even if you don't – the gravity will pull you back!

Some neutron stars are known as pulsars. They spin so fast that the whole star can turn 360° in less than a second. And they blast out beams of radio waves like whirling flashing space sirens.

But there is one type of neutron star that makes that seem rather relaxing. I'm talking about the mean, murderous magnetar.

The magnetar is like a giant magnet – but you wouldn't want one on your fridge. If a magnetar was where the moon is, its force would rip away every bit of magnetic metal on Earth and wipe clean your dad's classic music cassette collection. And that's the nice bit…

The fearsome force would turn all the humans on Earth into slime soup by re-arranging every bit of matter in their bodies. And that really is no laughing matter!

But, for really big stars – those weighing more than 20 Suns – an even more frightening future is in store. Something that makes the magnetar look warm and fluffy. With these really big stars, the bit left after the supernova blast shrinks into … A HORRIBLE BLACK HOLE! Visiting a black hole could spoil your "hole" day – but if you wanna try it…

Horrible Holidays present…

The Black Hole Hotel

Why not "drop-in" for a "hole" lot of fun?! It's more than just a hole, it's a hole in the universe. And you'll find its pull hard to resist! Once inside, you'll enjoy a quick break! Well, several breaks, as your body is pulled into long stringy bits and squished smaller than a pinhead and never seen again…
You'll be thrilled to bits…

YES, VERY LITTLE BITS!

Oh, so you don't fancy spending your holidays in a hole? And you'd rather clean a toilet with your toothbrush... Oh well, cheer up!

There's a star in every body!

You see, those exploding giant stars aren't all bad news. Bet you never knew that much of your body is made of bits of blown-up stars! Here's your very own incredible insides story...

Like every other star, giant stars spend time happily crunching hydrogen into helium. But not always. When the giant star is overheating and about to go pop, it crushes more and more bits of matter together and starts churning out other substances. The oxygen in your lungs, the iron in your blood and the carbon in your body were all made by an exploding star billions of years before you were born.

And now, at long last, it's your chance to have stars in your eyes. Yes, folks – it's star-staring time!

The Horrible Science Staggering Stargazers' Club

Every night sees the most eye-popping show in the universe. It's called the stars and here's your chance to join a brainy band of star spotters who are setting out to explore the universe using their eyeballs. Welcome to the Staggering Stargazers' Club!

Stuff needed for stargazing

A PAIR OF EYEBALLS

WARM CLOTHING, SUCH AS THICK SOCKS AND THAT EMBARRASSING SCARF YOUR GRANNY KNITTED

A CLEAR, DARK NIGHT WHEN IT'S NOT TOO WINDY

A NOTEBOOK AND PENCIL

A PAIR OF BINOCULARS OR A TELESCOPE (BUT THEY'RE NOT VITAL)

HORRIBLE SCIENCE
SPACE
STARS AND JUJU MUMMS

THIS BOOK

AN ADULT

DIM TORCH — IT CAN HELP YOU READ THIS PAGE WITHOUT HAVING TO WAIT AFTERWARDS FOR YOUR EYES TO GET USED TO THE DARK

A GARDEN CHAIR AND BLANKET (NOT VITAL)

IMPORTANT NOTE

Don't leave home without your adult. Also, do remember that adults get scared easily so don't wander off and leave them!

Here's what to do…

1 Take your equipment (including your adult) to a dark place away from street lights.

2 Look up at the sky. If you sit in the garden chair you can pretend to sunbathe – or should I say "star-bathe"? If you feel cold, you can snuggle under the blanket.

Got all that? Great!

Here's our first space spectacle coming right up!

A quick tour of the galaxy without leaving home

1 Take a look at the constellation (star pattern) of Orion. It's the one that looks like this. (The best time to see it is after Christmas.)

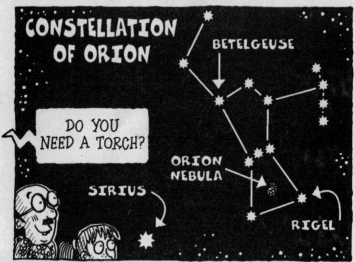

2 Can you see Sirius – the brightest star in the sky? It's about 8.6 light years away from us and 23 times brighter than the Sun. The only reason why you're not screaming, "AARGGGGH ME EYEBALLS!" is that Sirius is so far away, not much of its light is reaching us.

3 Now back to Orion... Stars can be different colours. Cooler stars can be red and hotter stars are bluish-white. Most star colours are too faint to see clearly, but you can see some in Orion if you look carefully:

- Rigel is a giant, hot, blue-white star. It's 900 light years away and 100,000 times brighter than the Sun.
- Betelgeuse is cooler than the Sun, but 800 times bigger and 10,000 times brighter. Luckily, it's about 650 light years away. It's a "red supergiant" star. You might be

able to see its tasteful orangey-colour. It's a kind of gruesome glimpse into the future of our Sun at the end of its life when it'll swell up and fry the Earth to a frazzle. (See page 137 for the red-hot details.)

- The Orion Nebula looks like a little twinkling cloud – you'll only see it if the sky's really dark. It's over 1,300 light years away and is part of a bigger, darker cloud that's 100 light years across. It's a sort of nursery where cute little baby stars are born – you can even see the baby stars twinkling. Who's a pretty baby then?

Note to readers in the southern half of the Earth
Orion can be seen from all over Earth except for the South Pole. But in countries south of the Equator, it'll appear upside-down compared to how it's shown here. So you could put the map upside-down. Or if you want to do things the hard way you could stand on your head to stare at the stars!

And instead of looking for Sirius, you might like to check out Canopus. It's here:

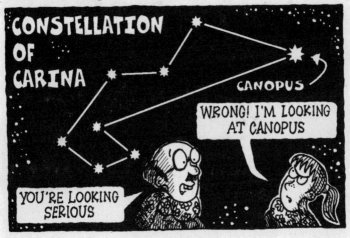

This giant star is 12,000 times brighter than the Sun and so far away its light takes 300 years to reach us. And that's a long way to come for a flying visit. So long! Have FUN!

Bet you never knew!
In 2001, astronomers found a huge boozy-woozy cloud of alcohol drops floating near the centre of our galaxy. Certain sozzled scientists are now trying to book spaceflights to get there.

But we're not. You see we're heading for the most important star of all. It's the star at the centre of our Solar System and the star we all depend on for light and heat. And if you "tan" the page, you'll find that the next chapter is a red-hot read!

The Sun is an ordinary, yellow star like millions more in the Milky Way. But it's still powerful and stunning. And the stunning Sun's sunshine is incredibly important for all of us on Earth…

Six stunning Sun statistics

1 The Sun is so hot that a pinhead heated in its centre would give off enough heat to kill a person 160 km away. STUNNING!

2 Imagine an iceberg 2.5 cm thick. The Sun's hot enough to melt the ice in 2 hours and 12 minutes, even though the iceberg is 150 million km from the Sun.

But just think… The Sun blasts heat in all directions all the time.

So imagine that you built a wall of ice 2.5 cm thick around the Sun at a distance of 150 million km.

Even though your wall would be 949 MILLION km long – the Sun could melt it *all* whilst you're enjoying a nice film. SCORCHING!

3 Every second, the sizzling Sun guzzles 564 million tonnes of its hydrogen fuel. I bet its gas bills are gigantic! Every minute, 235 million tonnes of hydrogen turn into energy. That's equal to ONE MILLION elephants blowing up every second! SENSATIONAL!

4 The Sun (and the Solar System, including us) are spinning around the centre of the Milky Way at something like 230 km a second. Reckon that sounds fast? It is. But it still takes 225 million years to do one lap – called a cosmic year. So far, the Sun's managed 20 laps – so it's 20 cosmic years old. STAGGERING!

5 The Sun "sings". Yes – *really*! The Sun's surface wobbles in and out. Waves of wobbling pass over the Sun's surface like the waves of air called sound waves. Sadly we can't hear the Sun's song. There's no air to carry the sound and, anyway, it's too deep for our Earthling ears to hear. But scientists have used a computer to make a similar sound and then made the sound higher-pitched so we can hear it. It's a deep rumbling noise – like a hungry hippo with a grumbling tum. SURPRISING!

6 The Sun gives off radio waves. These are just another form of energy, like light or radiation. Maybe the singing Sun could cut a single and play it on its own radio station? SHATTERING!

But the most stunning Sun fact of all is that without the Sun's heat and light, it would be night all over Earth for ever. It would soon start to get very cold and all the plants would die. And then all the animals that live off plants would die too and we humans would have nothing to eat. It doesn't bear thinking about – as any bear will tell you...

But despite the fact that the Sun is so obvious and important, we can't look at it...

Hmm – the Sun sounds a bit dangerous. And now for the next episode of our sci-fi space story. Will the aliens get sizzled by the stunning Sun?

Oddblob's Alien Adventure

We set off for the boring, yellow star known as the Sun. I told the Snotties that we wouldn't get too close to the star. If we did, our flying saucer would turn into a frying saucer, *snirk snirk**. Instead, my plan was to keep a safe distance and switch on our light filters so that we wouldn't get blinded.

On the way to the Sun, Sloppy became bored…

I had to explain that the Sun is easy to see because it's large and bright (unlike Sloppy who is neither large nor bright). But as any super-intelligent Blurb knows, it's a long way away. Afterwards, Sloppy played a game of snotball with my pet robot blurbi-dog, Roverbot.

* Ha ha! in Oddblob's language.

BLURBI-DATA

BY COSMO THE COMPUTER

☀ **NAME:** The Sun

☀ **SIZE:** 1,392,000 km across

☀ **SIZE COMPARED TO EARTH:** One million times larger

☀ **GRAVITY COMPARED TO EARTH:** 28 times stronger

☀ **LENGTH OF DAY:** Like a planet, the Sun spins in space but takes 28 Earth days to turn round once

☀ **ATMOSPHERE:** Super-heated gas called the corona. Steer clear of it - it's 2 million$^\circ$C

☀ **WEATHER FORECAST:** It's going to be UNBEARABLY HOT. The Sun's surface is about 6,000°C and its centre is 15 million$^\circ$C! It's also going to be windy - but the wind isn't made of air. It's bits of atoms blasted from the Sun. There's also lots of deadly radiation.

☀ **TRAVEL TIPS:** Keep your distance. But if you must go close, wear super-thick blurbi-shades and sunscreen and make sure your spacecraft has a really thick heat shield.

As we hovered at a safe distance, I pointed out the most interesting sights.

- Bumpy bits – The surface of the Sun looks like a sweet Earth fruit called an orange. The bumps are the tips of rising currents of hot gas.

- Sunspots – Those simple-minded Snotties reckoned the Sun had snotty-pox spots! I told them they were sunspots – holes in the surface made by magnetic forces. They were 1,500°C cooler than the Sun's surface but still blistering hot!
- Solar flares – These are a bit like a Snotty's slimy sneeze only the snot is bits of hydrogen. They can reach Earth and knock out primitive Earthling electrical equipment. That's the flares, not the Snotties' sneezes, snirk, snirk.

WARNING BY COSMO!

Solar flares are hot enough to bake a Blurb. If my sensors spot one, I'll warn you. But beware - the flares zoom at 400 km a second. So you'd better move fast, Oddblob!

From 20 million km away, Cosmo's super-sensitive sensors scanned the Sun's insides…

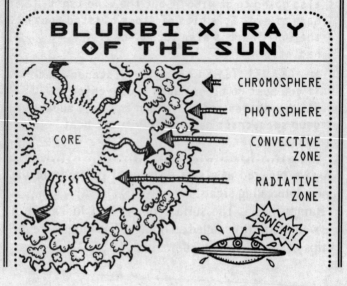

BLURBI X-RAY OF THE SUN

CORE

CHROMOSPHERE

PHOTOSPHERE

CONVECTIVE ZONE

RADIATIVE ZONE

SWEAT!

CHROMOSPHERE – This is the inner atmosphere. It's 10,000 km deep.

PHOTOSPHERE – This is the surface of the Sun. It's 300 km deep.

CONVECTIVE ZONE – This is the area where hot gases rise up from the core. It's 200,000 km deep.

RADIATIVE ZONE – 380,000 km thick.

CORE – 450,000 km across. Heat energy is made here.

It was too hot to go any closer to the Sun, but we did enjoy a blurbi-barbecue.

Now for a fascinating fact… The Sun makes up 99.86% of all the matter in our Solar System. It doesn't sound much – but the teeny leftover 0.14% includes the most incredibly interesting bits of the Solar System … the planets!

And right now we're off on a tour of the planets – from melting Mercury to perishing Pluto and all the weird worlds in between. So turn the page and climb aboard…

HOT AND HORRIBLE PLANETS

Anyone stupid enough to mess about on Mercury or visit Venus has less chance of escaping than a balloon in a pin factory. These planets are so hot and horrible that they would turn a person into goo in a fiery flash. You wouldn't send your worst enemy there … would you?

Here we goo…

A suffering scientist has been sent to Mercury by her worst enemy. She soon discovers that the planet moves in a weird way with an eerie effect on the days…

MY TRIP TO MERCURY by Ivana Coldrink (sorry about the scorch marks)

I arrived on Mercury this morning just in time to watch the Sun rise. It climbed in the sky and as it climbed it seemed to get bigger.

Around noon, I was about to eat my sandwiches when I noticed that the Sun had started to move backwards. I was so surprised that I forgot to eat, and my sandwiches turned into burned toast.

A little later, the Sun changed its mind and went forwards again. At the end of a very long day, it set in the evening but now it's reappeared! Suffering space rocks! What's going on?

Oh well, Ivana – you've got to suffer for science and this science sounds seriously scintillating. Here's what's happening…

So what's up with the Sun?

As Mercury orbits the Sun, it travels in a shape called an ellipse. It looks like this…

When Mercury is closer to the Sun – the Sun looks bigger. When the planet moves away from the Sun – the Sun looks smaller. And because a day on Mercury lasts 59 Earth days – and that's most of a Mercury orbit (88 Earth days) – the Sun can change size during one day. With me so far? Great! Now for the backwards bit…

On Earth, the Sun appears to cross the sky every day as the planet spins in space. But just imagine if our planet were spinning a lot slower. Well, then the Sun would seem to move slower. And if our orbit were faster than the speed the Sun seemed to move, the Sun would appear to go backwards. That's what happens with the slowly spinning Mercury! See what I mean?

Hmm – Mercury sounds mad. Oh well, let's catch up with our space story and see if Oddblob can make sense of mixed-up Mercury...

Oddblob's Alien Adventure

We set off for Mercury. It's the closest planet to the Sun – a quick hop of about 58 million km.

BLURBI–DATA

🌑 **NAME:** Mercury

🌑 **SIZE:** 4,900 km across

🌑 **SIZE COMPARED TO EARTH:** Three times smaller across

🌑 **GRAVITY COMPARED TO EARTH:** A little over one-third. That means you would be one-third your Earth weight, Oddblob.

🌑 **MOONS:** None

🌑 **LENGTH OF DAY:** 58 Earth days and 12 hours

🌑 **LENGTH OF YEAR:** 88 Earth days

🌑 **ATMOSPHERE:** Hardly any

🌑 **WEATHER FORECAST:** Too hot AND too cold. During the day it's 427°C – that's hot enough to melt a tin of blurbi-baked beans. And there's no escape from the Sun's radiation. At night, it's -183°C.

🌑 **TRAVEL TIPS:** It's not a sensible place to go – but if you really must visit Mercury, you'll need your spacesuit, your blurbi-shades and extra-thick thermal socks for those long cold nights.

As we swooped over Mercury, I pointed out the main tourist attractions. This didn't take very long as there weren't many.

- Cliffs – 3 km high.
- The Caloris Basin – a crater 1,300 km across.
- The deep craters have ice in them.

The Snotties pestered me to let them go skating in the craters. But I decided to move on 50 million km to Venus. I hoped it would be more interesting. And it was, but not in a nice way…

BLURBI-DATA

🌑 **NAME:** Venus

🌑 **SIZE:** 12,100 km across

🌑 **SIZE COMPARED TO EARTH:**
A bit smaller

🌑 **GRAVITY COMPARED TO EARTH:**
A little weaker

🌑 **MOONS:** None

🌑 **LENGTH OF DAY:** 243 Earth days

🌑 **LENGTH OF YEAR:** 225 Earth days. No, Oddblob I am not blowing my blurbi-chips! The planet spins so slowly that one Venus day lasts longer than one Venus year! And just to confuse you a bit more – Venus spins backwards compared to all the other planets…

🌑 **ATMOSPHERE:** Choking clouds of carbon-dioxide gas. This gas is poisonous. The atmosphere is heavy enough to crush you flat and the clouds are full of acid that could dissolve what's left of you.

Then there are the volcanoes... they're not erupting at present - but they might start at any moment.

○ **WEATHER FORECAST:** Today's going to be hot, 500°C to be exact, just the same as every day. It's the hottest place in the Solar System (not counting the Sun).

○ **TRAVEL TIPS:** I'd rather crash my computer chips than go to Venus!

Despite Cosmo's advice, I decided to land, even if we stayed in the spacecraft. But the Snotties wanted to go outside…

At this point Roverbot decided to go walkies…

46

This gave me the chance to point out the dangers of…

After I'd rescued Roverbot with the spacecraft's robot arm, he seemed rather upset and took it out on me…

But if Venus the planet is vicious and violent, Venus the god was vile! The Mayan people of Central America thought the planet was a god (not a goddess as the ancient Greeks believed). And Mayan priests spent lots of time looking at the planet to see what their god was up to. Was he moving? What time of day did he appear?

Could you be a Mayan astronomer?

This quiz is based on real events. It's the year 562. You're the priest astronomer to King Sky-witness of Calakmul. But are you an awesome astronomer or a feeble fortune-teller?

Here are the rules:

Read each question and decide on your answer. If you get it right, award yourself a point. Then move on to the next question.

1 It's 29 April. You know that on this day Venus will appear to stand still in the sky. What do you tell the king?

a) It's a good day to bash your enemies.

b) It's a good day to do a bit of shopping.

c) It's a bad day – you'd best go to bed and hide under the duvet.

Answer:

a) The god Venus is in charge of war and disaster. If he's hanging about in the sky (as seen from Earth) it's a good time to ask for his aid.

---

2 The king's army captures the rival city of Tikal with its king, Double Bird. What do you do with him?

a) Lock him in a small room and make him do hard sums.

b) Agree with him that life is very unfair and let him go.

c) Crush him under a wheel-shaped rock and cut his heart out.

Answer:

c) He was a sacrifice – a little thank-you prezzie for Venus.

48

3 Also captured was a royal prince named Animal Skull. He's only a boy. What do you do with him?

a) Drown him in a pot of custard. Then eat the custard.

b) Make him king and excuse him from going to school.

c) Tikal, I mean *tickle* him to death with a feather duster.

Answer:
b) But the boy has to do what you tell him to.

4 What do you do with King Double Bird's army?

a) Treat them to a slap-up supper.

b) Pull out their fingernails and cut out their hearts.

c) Send them to work in the royal chocolate factory.

Answer:
b) Venus likes sacrifices – he's a real "hearty" character.

What your score means...

0-1 You're far too nice to be a Mayan astronomer.

2-3 You might act a bit strangely if you had a stone heart-cutting knife in your hands. You're not a science teacher by any chance?

4 You're a menace to society and you'd make a great Mayan astronomer.

If you really want to be a Mayan astronomer, here's your chance to view Venus with your own eyeballs. (Just leave the stone knives at home!)

The Horrible Science Staggering Stargazers' Club

Don't forget the things you need from page 31!

Viewing Venus

Here's what to do…

1 Look out for Venus in the west, two hours after sunset. (You should be able to see the planet for about half the year – so if it's not there it'll turn up in a few months.)

2 Venus looks like a brilliant bright star. It's so bright because the Sun's light reflects off the planet's deadly choking clouds. Isn't that pretty?

Did you find Venus easily? Hopefully you did. But, in the past, viewing Venus has presented plenty of puzzling problems. It even wrecked some astronomers' lives.

This is the story of poor Guillaume Le Gentil. In 1761, this French scientist was keen to see a transit of Venus. That's when the planet moves across the face of the Sun as seen from Earth. With me so far?

For astronomers, a transit is something special. It's the chance of a lifetime to measure how big and far away Venus is compared to the Sun. A transit was due in 1761 and the best place to see it was India – so Guillaume sailed off to India. But his plans flopped faster than a bungee-jumping hippopotamus. If Guillaume had sent his scientific buddies letters they might have sounded like this (complete with a dodgy French accent)…

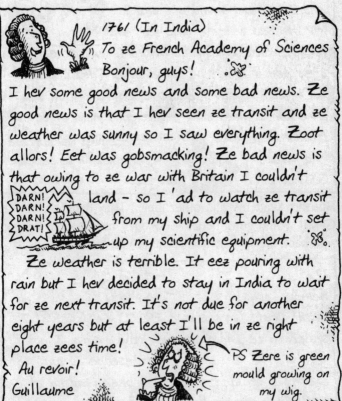

1761 (In India)
To ze French Academy of Sciences
Bonjour, guys!

I hev some good news and some bad news. Ze good news is that I hev seen ze transit and ze weather was sunny so I saw everything. Zoot allors! Eet was gobsmacking! Ze bad news is that owing to ze war with Britain I couldn't land – so I 'ad to watch ze transit from my ship and I couldn't set up my scientific equipment.

DARN!
DARN!
DARN!
DRAT!

Ze weather is terrible. It eez pouring with rain but I hev decided to stay in India to wait for ze next transit. It's not due for another eight years but at least I'll be in ze right place zees time!

Au revoir!
Guillaume

PS Zere is green mould growing on my wig.

After seven years of waiting, Le Gentil did some calculations. To his dismay, he found that he'd get a better view from Marianas Island in the Pacific Ocean. So he set off for the island as soon as he could. But, once again, his luck was out…

1769

Bonjour, guys!
Darn! Darn! Darn! I em in
Manila in ze Philippine Islands
and I hev just found out zat I
hev meesed ze only ship zat goes
to Marianas Island. I asked when ze next one
goes and it won't be for another THREE years!
  Oh well, mustn't grumble, as ze British say.
I reckon I weel still get a good view of ze
transit from 'ere.
  Au revoir!
Guillaume

I em 'ere

PS Ze bugs hev eaten a
huge hole in ze backside
of my trousers.

But the Academy had other ideas. They decided that Le
Gentil would get a better view back in India. So he was
sent back the way he had come – with fateful results…

1769

Bonjour, guys!
Darn! Drat! Curses and FRILLY KNICKERS! I
sailed to ze India like you told me to. I got
zere in time. I set up my telescope. I was so
excited I couldn't sleep. I'd been waiting
EIGHT long years for zees! Ze next
day ze Sun was shining. I was all
ready for ze transit and then… ze sky
clouded over and I did nat see a thing!
And now I hev just 'eard zat in Manila where

I wanted to stay zere was a blue sky and everyone saw the transit. And the next transit isn't due for another 100 years! ARRGGGH! I em jumping up and down on my mouldy wig!

Yours crossly
Le Gentil

1770

Bonjour, guys!

You do remember me – don't you? Eez me – Guillaume and I'm home! I hed a terrible voyage back from India. Well, it was three voyages actually – I kept getting shipwrecked. My trousers are all cut to pieces and my wig is washed overboard.

Well, when I got 'ome, everyone thought I was dead and my 'orrible family were just dividing up all my belongings.

Au revoir
Guillaume

PS My family says I should thank my lucky stars I em still alive. Grr – don't mention ze stars or planets or I will scream –ARGH!

Oh dear... Well, you'll have no trouble seeing this next planet. You probably see it every day and you might well be an expert on it! Yes, it's time to get down to Earth!

DOWN TO EARTH!

If I were an alien looking for somewhere to live, I'd certainly choose Earth. After all, it's the only planet with running water, air and the chance of finding a decent pizza. But enough of me – it's time for another episode of our slimy space story. Let's find out what the aliens think of Earth…

Oddblob's Alien Adventure

Earth would be a perfect planet to live on if it weren't overrun by those annoying half-witted humans. Mind you, when we landed on Earth, the Snotties acted almost as half-wittedly as the humans…

BLURBI-DATA

🌍 **NAME:** Earth

🌍 **SIZE:** 12,700 km across

🌍 **MOONS:** One – the Moon

🌍 **LENGTH OF DAY:** 24 Earth hours

🌍 **LENGTH OF YEAR:** 365.25 Earth days

🌍 **ATMOSPHERE:** 78% nitrogen, 21% oxygen. The rest is other gases including 0.5% carbon dioxide

🌍 **WEATHER FORECAST:** It's going to be hot around the Earth's middle and well below freezing at the poles (each end). A large amount of water will fall from the sky in the form of small drops. Earthlings call this rain.

As we approached Earth, I pointed out a couple of interesting features...

• Earth is mostly blue because of its water – 71% of the planet is covered in masses of water known as seas. Even the clouds are made of tiny drops of water floating in the air. As usual, the half-witted humanoids have got it wrong – they should be calling their planet Water rather than Earth or maybe Planet Damp and Drippy, snirk, snirk.

• Earth teems with life. You can see it from space – for example, huge areas of land are covered in giant green life forms known as trees. Despite their size, trees do not appear to be dangerous and have never been known to chase anyone.

WE COME IN PEACE!

Slobslime and Sloppy had never seen Earth's life forms and they hadn't been listening to my talk on trees ...

55

Then Slobslime met her first human.

The human had a dangerously fierce Earth creature with her…

On Earth, there are billions of tiny life forms called microbes – these can cause disease. Slobslime seemed to have fallen ill.

Well, I think Earth's lovely. OK, so I'm biased, but everyone who sees Earth from space is amazed at how pretty the planet looks with its shiny blue seas and its fluffy white clouds. Earth reflects so much sunlight it seems to glow in the dark...

Here's what astronaut Jim Lovell said back in 1968:

The vast loneliness up here is awe-inspiring, and it makes you realize just what you have back on Earth. The Earth from here is a grand oasis in the big vastness of space.

Earth's ultimate secret

Apart from its beauty, you might not think that Earth's that special. Of the nine planets in our Solar System, it's the third hottest planet with the fifth-fastest spin. It's the fifth heaviest planet and it has the fourth-strongest gravity. So what makes the Earth so special?

Notice anything?

Earth's in the middle of every list! Being the Solar System's Mr Average is what makes Earth special! It means that Earth isn't too hot or too cold for life. And it means that Earth's gravity is just right for all the life forms that live on it.

Including you and me.

But it doesn't stop there. Earth has other fantastic features that make it safe for life. My shady pal, Honest Bob, has moved into the second-hand planet business and he's keen to sell you the Earth. Can you spot what's wrong with his advert?

We'll be back after this commercial break...

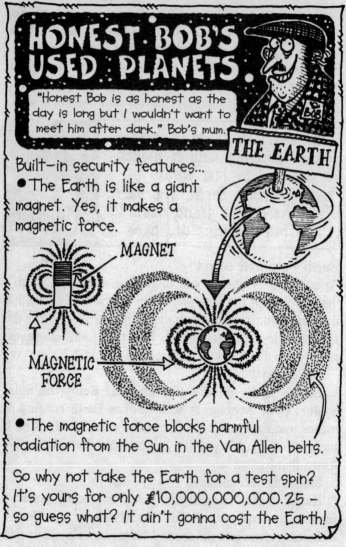

HONEST BOB'S USED PLANETS

"Honest Bob is as honest as the day is long but I wouldn't want to meet him after dark." Bob's mum.

THE EARTH

Built-in security features...

● The Earth is like a giant magnet. Yes, it makes a magnetic force.

MAGNET

MAGNETIC FORCE

● The magnetic force blocks harmful radiation from the Sun in the Van Allen belts.

So why not take the Earth for a test spin? It's yours for only £10,000,000,000.25 – so guess what? It ain't gonna cost the Earth!

So would you buy the Earth off Honest Bob? Hope not! As far as I know, the Earth isn't actually for sale! Let's ask Luke Upwards about the rest of Honest Bob's claims...

HONEST BOB IS BEING SURPRISINGLY... HONEST. ALL THE DETAILS HE GIVES ARE CORRECT!

Honest Bob was right about the Earth's defences against the Sun. But what's this? It looks like Izzie Starrs who works with Luke has a joke she wants to share with us…

WHERE DO YOU FIND THE VAN ALLEN BELTS?

IN SPACE?

ROUND VAN ALLEN'S TROUSERS!

PATHETIC!

Bet you never knew!
The Van Allen belts, named after US scientist James Van Allen who found them in 1958, are between 1,000 and 25,000 km from Earth. The Sun's radiation gets trapped by the Earth's magnetic field in the belts. But if a spacecraft broke down there, the astronauts would be revoltingly roasted by the radiation.

Now let's take Honest Bob up on his offer to take the Earth for a spin. We can because…

Shock horror news! Earth is moving!

Right now, you're whizzing through space at about 30 km a second (that's about 108,000 km an hour) as Earth whizzes around the Sun. In fact you've actually whizzed 300 km since the start of this sentence. And what's more, you, me, the cat and the goldfish and the entire Earth are *spinning* too!

How to enjoy a free round-the-world trip without getting out of bed

All you have to do is stay in bed all day at a point on the equator (the imaginary line around the Earth's middle). As the Earth spins in space you'll move with it. In one day, you'll travel a distance equal to going around the world. That's right – you enjoy a free 40,000 km space ride at 1,670 km an hour, *without getting out of bed!*

Now let's imagine you pushed your bed to the North Pole (or the South Pole if you prefer sleeping upside-down. Just make sure that duvet's really thick!) While you stay in bed all day, your bed will go around in a little circle like an ice skater in a tight spin. Confused? Hopefully this will help:

If you're at the North Pole, you can look up and see the Pole Star directly above your head. All the other stars seem to go around it in a circle as the Earth spins in space. Of course – you don't have to go to the North Pole to see the Pole Star. Anywhere in the northern half of the Earth will do...

The Horrible Science Staggering Stargazers' Club
First collect the things you need from page 31!
Peer at the Pole Star
Here's what you have to do...
1 Head for a dark place away from street lights.
2 Look up at the sky. Find the constellation called the Big Dipper or the Plough. The lovely romantic star names in the Plough are Arabian.

CONSTELLATION OF THE BIG DIPPER

DUBHE

ALCOR MIZAR MEGREZ

ALIOTH

ALKAID MERAK

PHEKDA

HOW ROMANTIC!

LOOKS LIKE A SAUCEPAN, TO ME!

Follow the line from Merak to Dubhe upwards and you're peering at the Pole Star.

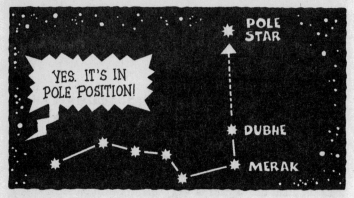

3 Can you see Alcor? It helps if it's a dark night! A thousand years ago the Arabs reckoned that you had good eyesight if you could spot Alcor.

4 The Pole Star is a giant star 2,000 times brighter than the Sun but, as luck would have it, it's a nice safe 480 light years away.

5 Since the star always appears directly over the North Pole – you can always tell which direction is north, even at night!

Bet you never knew!
Earth's spin has an embarrassing wobble. And that means by the year AD 14,000 the North Pole will be pointing to a different star. DRAT – this book will be out of date! But after another 12,000 years, we'll be pointing at the Pole Star again and you can blow the dust off this book and read it again!

Hold on – if you live in the southern half of the Earth you may be a bit miffed because you can't see the Pole Star. Don't be cross – you can stare at the Southern Cross instead!

The Horrible Science Staggering Stargazers' Club

Check out the Southern Cross

1 Here's where to look for it…

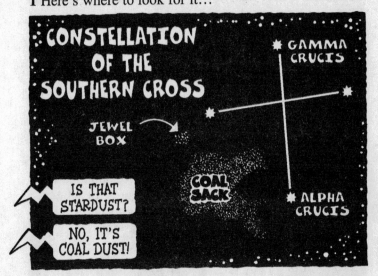

2 If the long arm of the cross were five times longer, it would end up above the South Pole.

3 Now here's a shock (I don't think). The Coal Sack is nothing to do with dirty lumps of coal and you won't find jewels in the Jewel Box. The Coal Sack is a big, dark cloud of gas and the Jewel Box is a group of distant stars.

Mind you, it doesn't matter where you live in the world – there's one thing in space everyone can see. Yes – you'd better turn that page fast or we'll miss our flight to the Moon!

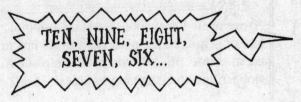

THE MADDENING MOON

The Moon's story started four billion years ago when the Earth got hammered on the head by a small planet and the weather changed. And here's the whole head-banging history...

The big bash

When Earth was whacked by a Mars-sized planet, the big bash blasted red-hot rocks into space. Gravity grabbed the rocks and rolled them into a ball and – BINGO! – the Moon was made. And that's how the seasons started too.

You see, Earth was knocked off balance and ever since it's been leaning over at an interesting angle of 23.44°.

So when the Earth goes round the Sun, the northern and southern halves of the planet take it in turns to lean towards the Sun and have summer. And now we've got the seasons sorted, it's time for another instalment of our slimy sci-fi story...

Oddblob's Alien Adventure

As we neared the Moon, I asked Cosmo the computer for some info on the place. But first I had to clean the green slime off his computer chips. Grrr – those slobbering slime-slopping Snotties!

BLURBI-DATA

⊙ **NAME:** The Moon

⊙ **SIZE:** 3,476 km across

⊙ **SIZE COMPARED TO EARTH:** A quarter its width

⊙ **GRAVITY COMPARED TO EARTH:** One sixth

⊙ **LENGTH OF DAY:** Nearly 28 Earth days

⊙ **LENGTH OF YEAR:** 365 Earth days and 6 Earth hours

⊙ **ATMOSPHERE:** Nothing much...

⊙ **WEATHER FORECAST:** The weather's going to be either too hot or too cold. During the day it's 110°C and blasted by radiation from the Sun. At night, it's -170°C. But at least there'll be no rain because there's no water, and no wind because there's no air.

⊙ **TRAVEL TIPS:** Wear spacesuits and leave the umbrella in the spacecraft.

From space we had a great view of the Moon and I showed the Snotties the most interesting sights.

• Craters – The Moon's craters were made by crashing exploding space rocks. There are about 300,000 craters and those slug-brained Snotties tried to count them all. Some craters are thousands of metres deep and their bottoms never see the Sun. They could contain ice.

...EIGHT, NINE, TEN, ELEVEN, TWELVE, THIRTEEN, FOURTEEN...

DON'T BOTHER!

- The Earth – When you're on the Moon, the Earth looks much bigger and brighter than the Moon does when seen from Earth. This is because the Earth is bigger than the Moon.

THAT WHERE NASTY CAT LIVES, MUM.

DON'T REMIND ME!

- The "seas" – Sadly, these are silly Earthling names for masses of dark rock that melted when giant space rocks hit the Moon 3.8 billion Earth years ago. No chance of space surfing, I'm afraid!

Baby Sloppy heard me say "seas" and thought we were going to the seaside…

GWOODY! BIG BWEACH – ME WANNA MAKE SANDY-SNOT CASTLE… WHERE'S SEA?

Because the Moon is smaller than the Earth, the gravity is weaker. This means that everything weighs one-sixth of its Earth weight. This came as a surprise to the Snotties…

Hmm – the Moon sounds cool! Sadly, NASA has just told me that I'm too unfit to be an astronaut, so I guess I'm stuck looking at the Moon. Never mind – staring at the Moon can be loads of fun! Especially if you're a member of…

The Horrible Science Staggering Stargazers' club

Make eyes at the Moon

Things to look for…

1 What shape is it?

Possible shapes   CRESCENT   FULL   GIBBOUS

IMPORTANT SCIENCE NOTE
The shapes depend on the angle the Sun is shining on the Moon as it orbits the Earth. The new Moon appears as a skinny sliver so close to the Sun that it's hard to make out. And it grows into a big round Moon before shrinking back into a crescent.

2 What time is it?

The new Moon rises at sunrise and sets at sunset. When the Moon is waning (getting thinner) it rises at midnight and sets at midday.

The full Moon rises about sunset and sets about sunrise. So the higher the full Moon is in the sky the later it is.

3 Can you see any details?

Here are three things you can spot without a telescope…

COPERNICUS — A 90-KM-WIDE CRATER

IT'S VERY PEACEFUL HERE!

SEA OF TRANQUILLITY WHERE THE FIRST HUMANS LANDED IN 1969

TYCHO — A ONE BILLION-YEAR-OLD CRATER

Note to readers in South America, Australia, New Zealand and southern Africa

You'll see the Moon like this:

No matter where you are on Earth, you'll only ever see one side of the Moon. And no, it's not because the Moon doesn't want us to see the other side… It's because the Moon only turns once as it circles the Earth. To show how this works, Luke Upwards is sitting in my swivel chair as Izzie Starrs walks around him. Luke's pretending to be the Earth and Izzie's the Moon. Hey – you might like to try this at home too!

Like the Moon, Izzie makes one turn each time she goes around Luke. Hmm – in that time Luke ought to make 28 of the turns we call "days". I'll just whizz him round. OH YUCK! Luke's been space-sick!

Well, by now you may be feeling you've mastered some of the Moon's maddening mysteries. But does that make you an awesome astronomer? Or are you simply spaced-out? Find out with these cosmic quizzes…

Cosmic quiz – 1

Mad Moon scientists have come up with some incredibly idiotic ideas about the Moon. Which idea did I make up?

PEAR-SHAPED? HE MUST HAVE BEEN BANANAS!

1 William Pickering (1858–1938) and George Darwin (1845–1912): The Moon was thrown off the Earth as it spun in space billions of years ago. The hole left by the Moon is the Pacific Ocean.

2 Frédéric Petit (1810–1865): There are TWO moons, the second one is very small.

3 Peter Hansen (1795–1874): The Moon is pear-shaped.

4 Hans Hörbiger (1860–1931): The mountains on the Moon are made of ice. There have been lots of moons, but they crashed to Earth and wiped out the giants who lived there.

Answers:

1 TRUE And they weren't too wrong – as you'll remember from page 64.

2 TRUE In the 1850s a lot of annoyed astronomers got eye-strain searching for the second moon. No one's found it yet.

3 FALSE Wrong! Ha ha! As if the Moon was pear-shaped! NO – Peter Hansen said the Moon was egg-shaped and the end that we can't see is covered in jungle. So there!

4 TRUE He must have been as barking mad as a dog up a tree! Maybe that's why nasty Nazi leader Adolf Hitler hailed half-crazed Hans as the world's greatest scientist.

You might think that these theories were as daft as the man who ate the skin and threw away the banana. And, of course, you'd be right – but could *you* do any better?

Cosmic quiz – 2
Which two items have been found on the Moon?
a) Germs that normally live up your nose.
b) Dust that smells of garlic.
c) Multicoloured bits of glass.
d) Slimy green lettuce.

Answers:
a) Yes, OK, so germs don't *live* on the Moon but these germs were found hiding in a camera in 1969. The camera had been taken to the Moon by an earlier spacecraft. The germs had been sneezed there when the camera was loaded on Earth and they were none the worse for their holiday on the Moon.
b) No. Moon dust smells of gunpowder not garlic.
c) Yes. Most Moon dust is black and shiny – which is why the Moon appears to shine brightly. But Moon dust also contains tiny bits of coloured glass made from melted minerals.
d) No. But plants grow well in Moon dust (with added water and air). So who knows? One day we might see gardening programmes from the Moon featuring lunar lilies and crater chrysanthemums.

What's in a name?

The first scientist to peer at the Moon through a telescope, Italian super-scientist Galileo Galilei (1564–1642), thought the Moon had "seas". And he even gave these places names…

Seas that you might like to visit on the Moon…
- The Bay of Rainbows
- The Lake of Dreams

Seas that you might want to avoid…
- The Ocean of Storms
- The Marsh of Decay
- The Lake of Death

…IT'S EITHER THE MARSH OF DECAY OR THE LAKE OF DEATH!

LANDING CRAFT TO EARTH… WE'RE MAKING A CRASH LANDING… WHERE ARE WE HEADING?

GROAN!

The puzzling place-names torture test…

Certain places on the Moon and the planets are named after places and people from Earth. This is handy for staggering a scientist.

Questions to ask…

1 ARE THE ALPS IN EUROPE?

"Yes," they say – quite rightly, since the Alps *are* in Europe.

You say, "No, they're on the Moon!" This is also true, since the Alps *are* mountains on the Moon.

2 WHERE IS ARABIA?

ER...

If they say, "It's in the Middle East", you can say, "No, it's a desert on Mars." This is just as true. And now the quiz gets crueller…

3 IS BEETHOVEN ON MERCURY?

NO, YOU LITTLE IDIOT — HE'S DEAD AND BURIED!

You can say, "Not the famous composer – I mean the 644-km-wide crater." Mercury's craters are named after famous arty people and that's why Mark Twain and Leonardo da Vinci *are* on Mercury. Just to confuse your victim, you could add that Beethoven is also an asteroid.

I GUESS HE'S INTO HEAVY ROCK THESE DAYS!

OK, I GIVE IN!

Bet you never knew!

Many Moon craters were named by Italian astronomer Giovanni Riccioli (1598–1671). Riccioli christened craters after famous astronomers. The crafty crater namer gave himself and his scientist pal, Grimaldi, generously giant craters but he didn't like Galileo so he gave him a crumbling cruddy crater…

GRR — I RATE A GREATER CRATER!

Mind you, even the chilly dark side of the Moon is cosy and cheerful compared to our next stop. Living on this planet must be as jolly as a blocked drain. And is it really the home of monsters – or is that just an ugly rumour?

CAN'T BE ANY UGLIER THAN A SNOTTY

I HEARD THAT, ODDBLOB!

MONSTERS ON MARS?

Mars is the must-see planet for monster hunters. In this chapter, you'll stumble across monster scenery, monster stories and who knows what else? You might even find a few microscopic Mars monsters squirming and slithering over the next few pages...

Yes, there's something about Mars that really wakes folk up – it's even been known to work on people who haven't woken up for years. In 1997, people all over Earth watched a live TV broadcast from Mars on the Internet. No, they weren't glued to an alien TV station – a camera on the Sojourner space probe sent pictures that were transmitted on the Internet.

Actually the live show was more of a dead show. Nothing appeared to happen on Mars and there was nothing to see except hundreds of rocks and a pretty pink sky. There would have been more life in a graveyard at midnight, but even so, one billion people gazed at the scene in awestruck amazement.

The really exciting part of the mission was when a man named Brian Cooper used virtual-reality software to drive a radio-controlled robot car named Rocky about on MARS! Would you like a Rocky for Christmas?

See you after the commercial break.

Oh well, it was fun while it lasted. Sadly, I've just heard that spoil-sport NASA scientists won't let me drive a robot car on Mars. But if that's got you interested in visiting the planet, I guess you've got a choice…

a) You could hang about waiting for a manned flight – there'll be one in a few years and, who knows, they might let you come along for the ride.

OR

b) You could try this experiment now and get an idea of what to expect on Mars…

Dare you discover … how to cause a Martian dust storm?

You will need:

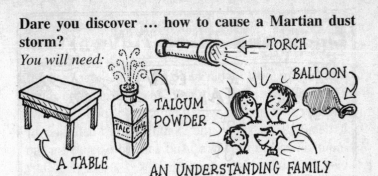

TORCH

BALLOON

TALCUM POWDER

A TABLE

AN UNDERSTANDING FAMILY

What you do:

1 Darken the room or wait until dark. Switch on the torch and place it so that it shines on the table from the side.

2 Sprinkle the table with talcum powder.

3 Blow up the balloon and let out the air a few times.

4 Now blow up the balloon and place the mouth of the balloon so that the escaping air blows over the top of the table.

You should notice:

The dust swirls out in a big cloud, billows into the air and floats about like a 100 per cent genuine Martian dust storm. Great, isn't it? In fact, just like on Mars, the dust storm starts when the wind blows bits of dust against each other that knock into more dust, etc.

> **WARNING TO YOUNGER READERS**
> *Ask permission before blanketing your home in a talcum powder dust storm. If you don't, you might be sent to Mars or possibly to your bedroom, until the dust settles!*

And now it's time for another slimy slice of sci-fi story action. This time the aliens explore Mars…

Oddblob's Alien Adventure

Mars is my most favourite planet in the Solar System! The scenery is massively more magnificent than Earth and there are no half-witted humans to spoil the view! I decided to show the Snotties the delights of mountaineering on Mars. And I asked Cosmo for the background basics…

BLURBI—DATA

◯ **NAME:** Mars

◯ **SIZE:** 6,800 km across

◯ **SIZE COMPARED TO EARTH:** Half Earth's diameter

◯ **GRAVITY COMPARED TO EARTH:** Not much more than one third as much

◯ **MOONS:** Deimos and Phobos – they're only a few km across

◯ **LENGTH OF DAY:** 24 Earth hours and 37 Earth minutes

◯ **LENGTH OF YEAR:** 687 Earth days

◯ **ATMOSPHERE:** Just a few wisps of carbon dioxide

◯ **WEATHER FORECAST:** It's going to be very cold (about -30°C) but at least it won't rain. After all, it hasn't rained for four billion years. There's a chance of a dust storm that could last days. Don't worry, Oddblob - the winds are weak because there's so little air. It won't be windy enough to blow you away.

◯ **TRAVEL TIPS:** Soil chemicals can dissolve your space boots and some of your 24 toes.

As we came in to land on Mars, I showed the Snotties the superb scenery…

GET A LOAD OF THIS LOT...

- The Mariner Valley is the vastest valley in the Solar System. It's 6.4 km deep and 241 km wide – four times deeper and six times wider than that crack in Earth known as the "Grand Canyon". It's long enough to stretch across the puny Earthling country known as the United States of America.
- There are river valleys and lakes where water flowed on Mars billions of years ago. Some rivers were more than 24 km wide and 100 metres deep.
- Deimos and Phobos were probably asteroids that were pulled in by the gravity of Mars. Phobos, the slightly larger moon, rises in the west and sets in the east and goes across the sky in 4.5 Earth hours. Deimos is so titchy it looks like a bright star.
- Mons Olympus is the Solar System's highest mountain. It's a volcano 483 km wide and 25 km high – twice as wide as Earth's widest volcano and three times as high as Earth's most massive mole-hill, I mean mountain.

THAT'S WHERE WE'RE GOING TO CLIMB!

GULP!

79

We decided to climb Olympus Mons starting at the top! Well, *really*! (Talk about tourists taking life easy – anyone would think they're on holiday!) To get enough energy, the Snotties snacked up on slime ice cream first.

Just then Sloppy decided she wanted to visit Deimos. Deimos is so small its gravity is very weak. We were almost weightless there!

Suddenly, Slobslime suffered a gut gas problem! In the weak gravity this was enough to blast her into space.

But Roverbot rushed to her rescue…

Five facts not many people know about Mars moons

1 The gravity in Deimos is so weak you can take off into space just by riding a bike. And Slobslime's super-strong bottom burp is sure to result in a blown-off blast-off.

2 If you want to see what Deimos looks like from Mars, try this exciting experiment. Ask a friend to hold a potato at one end of a football pitch. Seen from the other end of the football pitch, the potato looks the same size as Deimos as seen from Mars. Not very big, in other words. (If you're feeling cruel, you can wander off and leave your friend holding a potato for hours.)

3 Actually, Deimos even *looks* like a potato, although it won't make tasty French fries.

SPOT THE DIFFERENCE

POTATO

DEIMOS

4 Each time Phobos orbits Mars, it spirals lower – dropping 18 cm every 100 Earth years. In 40 million years, the moon is due to hit Mars with messy results for any humans or aliens living there at the time.

5 In the 1950s, Ukrainian scientist Iosif Shmuelovich Shklovskii said that the moons of Mars were made by super-smart Martians. But in 1971, US space-probe photos proved that Phobos was just a large rock and the red-faced scientist said that he'd been joking.

Alien invaders

So what about those alien invaders and Mars monsters? Well, at present, we aren't sure that there are aliens in the Solar System at all. But some past astronomers have been mad-keen on the idea of Mars aliens. And some of them thought there may be life on Venus too. But, as I'm sure you've guessed, these claims were a bit too barmy to be believable…

CHEEKY CLAIMS
by Barmy Boffins

TEDIOUS TRUTH
by Luke Upwards

1 Swedish scientist Svante Arrhenius (1859–1927) 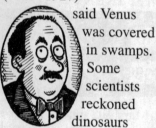 said Venus was covered in swamps. Some scientists reckoned dinosaurs could live there.

1 There's no water on Venus and it's hot enough to turn dinosaurs into instant tasty dino-dinners.

2 In the 1830s, German astronomer, Franz von Paula Gruithuisen said Venus appears brighter every 47 years because the aliens light lamps in honour of their new emperor.

2 You'll know why Venus shines from page 50. Scientists aren't too sure why the brightness changes (if it does). But it's nothing to do with alien emperors.

But those spaced-out scientific suggestions sound normal compared with the most crazy, cheesy alien claim ever!

THE NEW YORK SUN
27 August 1835

GIANT BEAVER BOUNDS ABOUT ON MOON!

Sir J.H.

Top astronomer Sir John Herschel has spotted a giant beaver on the Moon! "It walked on two feet and it didn't have a tail," gasped the awe-struck astronomer. Sir John said that the Moon is covered in trees and he's seen herds of hairy bison that waggle their ears, and ape-like humans with wings. "There's something unearthly about the whole scene – oh yes, silly me, that's because it's not Earth!" added Sir John.

OUR ARTIST'S IMPRESSION OF THE BEAVER

A MESSAGE FROM THE EDITOR

Gee-whizz, we'd sure like to thank all you folks who've been buying our paper. We were on the edge of going bust, but since we started reporting these Moon discoveries, we've become the biggest-selling paper on the planet – yee ha!

And the truth? The staggering stories had been cooked up by reporter Richard Adams Locke (1800–1871). The real Sir John Herschel was in South Africa. When he got to hear of the *Sun*'s tall tales, he was confused, but then he started to laugh very loudly.

But what about the Mars monsters?

Oh yes, thanks for reminding me! The most famous astronomer to believe in aliens on Mars was Percival Lowell (1855–1916). Now, as you can see from these dates, Percy's been pushing up the pansies for quite a few years. But I'm pleased to say that he's agreed to appear on the only TV show where the broadcast is live even if the guests are dead…

That planet you said existed beyond Neptune...

YES! I SPENT YEARS LOOKING FOR IT, BUT I COULDN'T FIND IT!

It was found in 1930 – we call it Pluto. And you know those canals you saw on Mars?

YES, THEY WERE DUG BY BRAINY ALIENS TO BRING WATER TO THE DESERTS ON MARS.

You know you built a special telescope to see them and spent years mapping them...?

Y-E-S?

You were seeing things! Spacecraft have landed on Mars and proved they don't exist!

THIS IS SO EMBARRASSING – I WISH I WAS DEAD!

You are dead!

The rotten reality is that when the two US Viking spacecraft landed on Mars in 1975 and 1976, they found that Mars is missing the basics for life. The sort of things you'd like to find in your home – warmth, water and air – don't exist on Mars. Trust Honest Bob to tell you the bad news – and sell you the planet into the bargain...

HONEST BOB'S USED PLANETS

"Honest Bob was a lovely kid – as long as he was asleep he did nothing wrong" – Bob's mum.

MARS

REALLY COOL!

IDEAL SIZE!

NO DAMP!

LOVELY COLOUR!

- OK, so it's got 4.6 billion years on the clock. But that's what you might call a genuine antique – and it's real old too!

- It's not too big! I mean, it's cosy – some folk don't like a big planet.

- Real smart red colour to it. I deny that it's rust. OK – so the rocks are a bit rusty – but hey, that's all part of its character.

- It's a bit cold, but as my mum always says, a bit of cold won't kill you. Well, it will, but it's kinda healthy too!

- OK, so the planet's kinda dry at present, but at least you won't get rising-damp problems.

Why not take a trip to Mars and look at it for yourself? You'll love it!

LOW COST!

At only £700,000,000.12 – I'm robbing myself (instead of robbing you – OOPS pretend I didn't say that!).

The truth about Honest Bob's claims...

Don't be fooled by all that claptrap about "cosy" Mars. The terrible truth is that Mars is too small for its own good. Billions of years ago, Mars had lots of air and water. The cosy air blanket kept Mars warm enough for running water. But because Mars is smaller than Earth, the planet's gravity wasn't strong enough to hang on to the air. Ultraviolet rays from the Sun split the water into gases that wafted off into space. And that's why a visit to Mars is presently as pleasant as a pyjama party in a deep freeze.

What's that, Luke?

Luke Upwards writes...

But give Bob his due - he's right about the rust. Iron in the rocks has rusted and that's why people call Mars "the red planet". If you get to see Mars from Earth, you'll find it even looks red from here!

So Mars isn't too nice right now – but is there any chance of life?

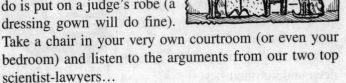

Surprisingly the answer isn't "NO", it's "hmm..." Well, that's what I think. But maybe you should judge for yourself? Yes, all you need to do is put on a judge's robe (a dressing gown will do fine). Take a chair in your very own courtroom (or even your bedroom) and listen to the arguments from our two top scientist-lawyers...

Putting the case for LIFE ON MARS is Izzie Starrs.

And putting the case against LIFE ON MARS is Luke Upwards.

Over to you, Luke!

Luke: Life on Mars? No way! I mean, there's no water and it's too cold. When the Viking spacecraft did robot tests on the soil, they couldn't prove that there was life.

Izzie: Objection, your honour! The tests showed chemical changes that might have been caused by microbes.

Luke: It was just a chemical reaction!

Time out to think it over: **WHAT DO YOU THINK?**

OK – now it's time for the case for life on Mars…

Izzie: So Mars is pretty dry now – but it once had lakes and rivers and where there's water, there's life. Maybe there's ice or even water deep underground.
And maybe there are microbes hiding there. Microbes on Earth aren't too fussy – they're at home in ice and deep underground.

MICROBES

Luke: Objection, your honour – she keeps saying "maybe"!

Time out: WHAT DO YOU THINK?

Izzie: In 1996, some scientists found fossil microbes in a rock from Mars. Here's exhibit A.

Luke: Objection! That's just a grotty old lump of rock. These so-called fossil microbes are too small to have been real microbes.

Izzie: But they could be hairs that the microbes used to swim about. Chemical changes in the rock could have been caused by microbes!

Time out: WHAT DO YOU THINK?

Luke: OK – you asked for this! In 1932 a scientist said he'd found microbes in a rock from Mars. They were found to be microbes from human snot. Here's Exhibit B.

Izzie: That's gross!

TIME FOR OUR LAWYERS TO SUM UP...

Luke: There's no way that there's life on Mars. Even if there were once life (and there's no proof), it doesn't mean there's life now!

Izzie: It's possible that rocks with microbes in them could have been blasted from Mars and landed on Earth and brought life to Earth. We might have started off as aliens from Mars!

Luke: Are you calling me an alien from Mars?

Izzie: Well, you're slimy enough!

Hey, break it up, guys! It's only science and there's nothing at stake except our whole understanding of life and the way we see our place in the universe. Er – OK, that sounds rather a lot. OOOH DEAR! I bet that hurt, Luke!

Bet you never knew!

In 1995, scientists Michel Mayor and Didier Queloz at Geneva University spotted a tiny wobble in the star called 51-Pegasi. They found out that this was caused by the gravity of a huge planet that was orbiting the star. Since then, scientists have found scores of planets. And many stars have planets like our own Solar System. (In 2003, they even found a planet that was about to be swallowed up and blasted by a giant star.) So all in all, there's a great chance of alien life lurking somewhere out there...

BUT THERE'S STILL NO PROOF!

A rocky road

I've got a feeling that the arguments in this chapter might run and run. Tell you what, let's make a run ourselves – for Jupiter! But wait, what's this… Someone's dumped a load of boulders in our way!

Remember those big space rock asteroid thingies? There are more than a million of them between Mars and Jupiter. And here's what they're about…

Slimy space fact file

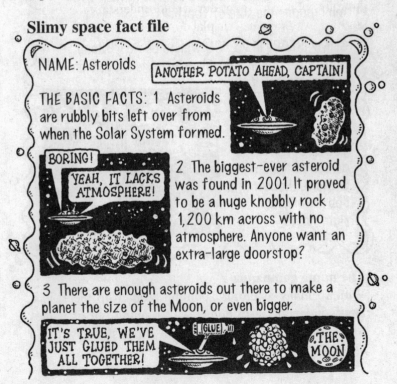

NAME: Asteroids

ANOTHER POTATO AHEAD, CAPTAIN!

THE BASIC FACTS: 1 Asteroids are rubbly bits left over from when the Solar System formed.

BORING!

YEAH, IT LACKS ATMOSPHERE!

2 The biggest-ever asteroid was found in 2001. It proved to be a huge knobbly rock 1,200 km across with no atmosphere. Anyone want an extra-large doorstop?

3 There are enough asteroids out there to make a planet the size of the Moon, or even bigger.

IT'S TRUE, WE'VE JUST GLUED THEM ALL TOGETHER!

GLUE

THE MOON

4 Unfortunately, Jupiter's gravity knocked the asteroids together and smashed them to bits so they didn't get the chance to make a planet. Poor little darlings!

5 In 2000, scientists found an asteroid shaped like a dog's bone.

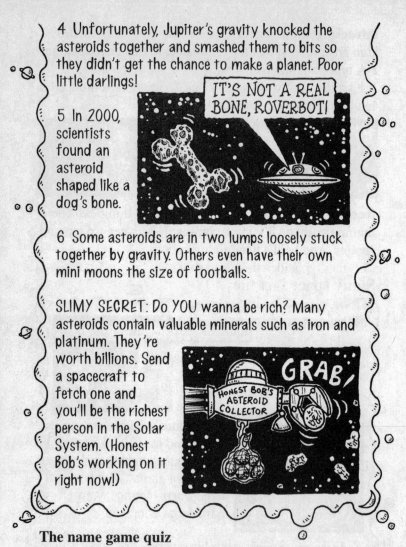

IT'S NOT A REAL BONE, ROVERBOT!

6 Some asteroids are in two lumps loosely stuck together by gravity. Others even have their own mini moons the size of footballs.

SLIMY SECRET: Do YOU wanna be rich? Many asteroids contain valuable minerals such as iron and platinum. They're worth billions. Send a spacecraft to fetch one and you'll be the richest person in the Solar System. (Honest Bob's working on it right now!)

HONEST BOB'S ASTEROID COLLECTOR

GRAB!

The name game quiz

With so many asteroids zooming around up there, is it any wonder that astronomers are running out of names for them! Which two items from this list *haven't* had asteroids named after them?

1 Mr Spock, the character from the 1960s TV series – *Star Trek*.
2 A type of pudding.
3 A shipping company.
4 A pop group.
5 A well-known brand of washing powder.

ASTEROID AND CUSTARD

YUMMY!

HUH?

MADE UP
1 There IS an asteroid called Mr Spock but it was named after an astronomer's ginger cat! The cat was named after the TV character – so you can have half a point if you said TRUE.
5 I guess this idea didn't wash with astronomers.

TRUE
2 Halawe is a sweet eaten in the Lebanon. It's a tasty blend of sugar, ground sesame seeds and lemon juice. But if you sink your teeth into Halawe the asteroid by mistake, your teeth will fall out!
3 Hapag was a German shipping company.
4 Yes, it's the only place in the universe that you can still see the famous 1960s pop group The Beatles together. So let's have a big cheer for asteroids Lennon, McCartney, Harrison and Starr. Shame they can't sing.

Phew – at last we're safely through the asteroid belt. Now for the big one. It's time to hit Jupiter! Well, let's hope we don't actually *hit* the planet. That might be a teeny-weeny bit fatal…

JUPITER

LET'S GO!

GIANT JUPITER AND SHOW-OFF SATURN

If Jupiter were human, he'd be a big bullying crook and the moons would be his gang. So, let's meet the roughest, toughest gangster gang in the Solar System.

THE JUPITER GANG

BIG J → EUROPA

IO →

CALLISTO GANYMEDE

Yes, Big J's a planet-sized bully. He's so awful, the cosmic cops are after him…

**THE MEMOIRS OF
DETECTIVE PLANET OF THE SSPD**
Yeah, I remember Big J. He was a nasty big-time crime boss over on the wrong side of the Solar System. You couldn't miss him - he had this big red spot on his face and I figure he'd been eating too many asteroids because his waist sure was bulging.

Now, Big J was a big, mean fella - I mean he had real gravity. He had a gang of four big moons. There are also loads of smaller moons, but they were small

fry – little more than
hangers-on. Anyhow, we got
complaints that Big J was
turning the heat on one
of his own gang members,
a moon called Io. Poor Io
was melting inside thanks
to Big J's gravity, helped out by the
rest of the gang. What a crowd of sickos!
Then the finger was pointed at Big J for
picking up asteroids by gravity and
firing them in the general direction of
Earth. Yessir – Jupiter was the meanest
critter I ever met in my years of cosmic
crime-fighting. He was always armed and
dangerous. He had a radiation gun. Hey –
don't ask me how it works, I'm just a
cop. Big J picked up radiation from the
Sun using some kind of magnetic force.
And this low-life scumbag planet blasted
all the moons around him! He even blasted
his next-door neighbour, Mr Saturn! The
best thing to do with Big J was to lock
him away and throw away the key!

Get the message?
Jupiter is more antisocial than a slug in a salad bar.

And now it's time for another incredible instalment of
our sci-fi space story. In their tour of the Solar System,
the aliens have reached Jupiter…

Oddblob's Alien Adventure

Jupiter is dangerous. The very idea of going there gave
both my brainy brains a hammering headache. But, for

some stupid reason, those half-witted Snotty space tourists wanted to take a closer look. Too close for safety!

BLURBI-DATA

🪐 **NAME:** Jupiter

🪐 **SIZE:** 140,000 km across

🪐 **SIZE COMPARED TO EARTH:** 1,321 times bigger

🪐 **GRAVITY COMPARED TO EARTH:** About 2.5 times stronger.

🪐 **MOONS:** Four big ones and loads of little ones - probably asteroids trapped by Jupiter's gravity

🪐 **LENGTH OF DAY:** Nine Earth hours and 51 Earth minutes

🪐 **LENGTH OF YEAR:** 11.8 Earth years

🪐 **ATMOSPHERE:** Mainly hydrogen with a bit of helium. My sensors detect hydrogen crushed by the pressure of gravity into a liquid. And there's nowhere to land.

🪐 **WEATHER FORECAST:** Hold on tight,

Oddblob - it's going to be stormy. One storm, the Great Red Spot, has been blowing for 300 years and I forecast it'll be blowing today. Don't think that you'll be safe away from the planet. The radiation around Jupiter is strong enough to blast a Blurb.

◎ TRAVEL TIPS: Avoid this planet!

> THAT'S WHY WE CAN'T GO THERE

And with that I pointed out the things we could see from a safe distance.

> ARE YOU **SURE** THIS IS A SAFE DISTANCE, ODDBLOB?

- Bulging middle – Jupiter spins so fast that it bulges a bit in the middle.
- Dark bands of clouds caused by areas of cooler gas that sink towards the planet.
- Great Red Spot – The winds in this stormy area are strong enough to flatten a skyscraper. Sometimes the spot turns grey – maybe Jupiter uses anti-spot cream, snirk, snirk.

SINK! SPIN! WHIRL! BULGE!

Hmm – bulging middle, big red spot. Jupiter reminded me of Slobslime, except she had a big green spot. By now, the Snotties had lost interest in Jupiter and were eyeing up Europa with all three of their eyes.

We decided to land on Europa for a spot of space skating. Snotties are fond of this sport because they can glide along without much effort…

At this very moment, an asteroid crashed into Europa and made a hole in the ice. And, of course, Slobslime fell in!

The ice is many kilometres thick, but beneath it there is an ocean up to 100 km deep. After Slobslime fell in, the ice quickly froze above her in the cold of space. There was only one thing we could do … and that was nothing!

In the end I had to rescue Slobslime to shut Sloppy up. So I fired the spacecraft's engine to melt the ice and grabbed Slobslime from the water.

The icy cold instantly froze Slobslime into a block of ice. And while she was melting I decided we'd all had enough of Europa.

IMPORTANT SCIENTIFIC NOTE

Scientists think that there might be life in Europa's ocean. There could be alien microbes or maybe giant worms (similar to worms that live in Earth's deep oceans). But Oddblob didn't even look for them... What a shame!

Amazing moons

Even without the worms, Jupiter's moons are awfully odd. So here's a really odd thought to amuse you. What would Jupiter moons *taste* like? Welcome to the Solar System's first cosmic cook book!

The Cosmic Cook Book

Hi to all you intergalactic gourmets! If you're feeling hungry, why not treat yourself to these tasty recipes … they're cooked just the way old Jupiter likes 'em!

Io pizza

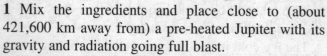

Ingredients:
Several million tonnes of rock
Sulphur (according to taste)
Hydrogen

1 Mix the ingredients and place close to (about 421,600 km away from) a pre-heated Jupiter with its gravity and radiation going full blast.
2 Leave for 4.6 billion years, while Jupiter cooks the mixture until the rocks melt.

WARNING ~ The mixture will get very hot (up to 500°C in places) and its insides will bubble up to the surface. They'll stink of rotting eggs but it's all part of the flavour!

Europa slushy-melt

Ingredients:
Several million tonnes of rock
Enough water to fill all of Earth's oceans
Alien microbe slime and giant worms
(if you like that sort of thing)

1 Form the rock into a ball and pour on the water.
2 Freeze until the outside is frozen solid but the inside is still runny.

For a more crunchy mixture, try the Callisto method.
You freeze the ice a little more and crack it a bit. Or
you can simply mix the rock and ice into a ball (the
Ganymede method).
It really is that simple.
Enjoy your moons
and *bon appetit*!

Oh, so you didn't fancy munching one of Jupiter's moons?
I guess it's time to make our escape from Jupiter and shoot
off to Saturn. And by some curious coincidence, the next
episode of our space story is set there...

Oddblob's Alien Adventure

Slobslime thawed out of her ice block in time to see
Saturn. Of course, the brainless alien was confused by
the rings.

> WOW — THAT'S
> AN EARTHLING
> IN A HAT!

With a big sigh, I asked Cosmo for the low-down on
Saturn. With an equally big sigh, Cosmo replied…

BLURBI-DATA

🪐 NAME: Saturn

🪐 SIZE: 120,500 km across

🪐 SIZE COMPARED TO EARTH: 764 times
bigger

GRAVITY COMPARED TO EARTH: Only 1.16 times as much. That's because Saturn is mostly made up of light gas with weak gravity. The whole planet is light enough to float on water!

MOONS: I had a dreadful job trying to count them. There are about 22 above 20 km in size, but there could be more that my sensors missed. The big one (5,150 km across) is called Titan

LENGTH OF DAY: 10 Earth hours and 38 Earth minutes

LENGTH OF YEAR: 29.5 Earth years

ATMOSPHERE: Hydrogen and helium, like Jupiter

WEATHER FORECAST: EXTREME WEATHER WARNING! The winds reach 1,800 km an hour. There's no solid surface to land on and there's a danger of being seasick or airsick or both. Probably at the same time.

TRAVEL TIPS: Take a giant windbreak and a large supply of sick bags.

We got a great view of Saturn's rings and I told the Snotties about how there were thousands of rings and how each one is made of shiny bits of ice and rock. They may have come from a crashed comet. Moons move between the rings and their gravity holds the rings together...

BITS OF ROCK AND ICE VARY IN SIZE!

Then I realized that the Snotties weren't listening.

I decided to wake up those snoring Snotties…

We Blurbs love blurbi-kite-flying. Unfortunately, the winds of Saturn proved just a bit too strong…

Lucky old Oddblob! Don't you wish you could see Saturn's rings close up? Of course, you can see the real thing if you happen to be looking through a really good telescope. But if you don't have a really good telescope, here's the next best thing:

Dare you discover ... Saturn's rings?

What you need:

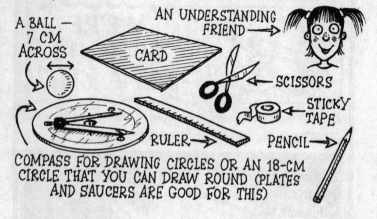

A BALL — 7 CM ACROSS

CARD

AN UNDERSTANDING FRIEND →

← SCISSORS

STICKY TAPE

RULER →

PENCIL →

COMPASS FOR DRAWING CIRCLES OR AN 18-CM CIRCLE THAT YOU CAN DRAW ROUND (PLATES AND SAUCERS ARE GOOD FOR THIS)

What you do:

1 Using the compass, or an object to draw round, draw a circle on the card 18 cm across. The circle should be 11 cm wider than the ball. Cut the circle out.

2 Cut out the inside of the card circle to make a card ring.

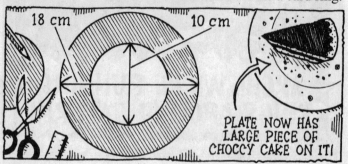

18 cm   10 cm

PLATE NOW HAS LARGE PIECE OF CHOCCY CAKE ON IT!

3 Stick your card ring to the ball with sticky tape.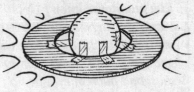

4 Well done, you've just made Saturn! Ask your friend to hold it in their hand and stand 15 metres away from you. They should start by holding the planet level and then at an angle.

You should notice:

When the rings are held level you can't see them. They're too thin and far away. The real Saturn's the same. Saturn spins at an angle, and every 15 years the rings cannot be seen from Earth. In fact, we're looking at Saturn sideways on.

But they appear when seen from any other angle…

That moon's the limit

But let's drag our eyeballs away from the rings. I've got some BIG news! Honest Bob's just sold me a ticket to the biggest night out in the Solar System. It's the Saturn's Odd Moons Awards. They're like the Hollywood Oscars in space!

SATURN'S ODD MOONS AWARDS

All the stars are out in force for this glittering galactic event! And the awards for the oddest moon prizes for Saturn are as follows...

THE CRAZIEST MOON couple award goes to ... **Janus** and **Epimetheus**. Hey, what's up with these guys? Every four years they swap orbits. Are they getting bored or something?

CRAZIEST MOON

UGLIEST MOON

THE UGLIEST MOON award goes to ... **Tethys**. This moon has a crack running halfway around it. Anyone know a planet plastic surgeon?

THE MOST TASTY-LOOKING MOON award goes to ... **Hyperion**. It's shaped like a giant hamburger. Fast food anyone?

THE BEST-DRESSED MOON award goes to ... **Iapetus**. This moon is wearing a lovely stripy black and white zebra-style outfit. Very trendy – give us a twirl!

And now for the one we've all been waiting for! The award for THE MADDEST MOON ON SATURN...

And the winner is ... **TITAN!** Yes, Titan's the looniest moon of all! Unlike every other moon in the Solar System, Titan's got a thick nitrogen-gas atmosphere. This atmosphere is orange. There may be seas of methane – a chemical found in cooker gas and cow farts. I guess Titan must be the ultimate moo-moon!

> I'D LIKE TO THANK EVERYONE WHO'S HELPED ME IN THE LAST FOUR BILLION YEARS, ESPECIALLY SATURN. JUST BECAUSE I'M −180°C SOME PEOPLE THINK I'M A BIT COLD. BUT I'M REAL FRIENDLY AND OFFER A WARM WELCOME, JUST SO LONG AS YOU DON'T MIND FREEZING TO DEATH.

And I do hope you don't mind a bit of freezing. You see, the remaining planets on our tour of the Solar System are chilly and cold with a c-c-capital C! D-dare you take a look?

YOU CAN BORROW ONE OF MY BLURBI BOBBLE-HATS!

The wonderful thing about the Solar System is that you can be really weird and wacky and way out and no one seems to mind. And they don't come weirder, wackier or further-out that those kooky, chilly planets – Uranus, Neptune and Pluto…

Take Uranus, for example. This planet is seriously way out. It's way out from the Sun by about 2,871 million km. And it's so weird and way out that instead of spinning, it tumbles head over heels through space like an out-of-control acrobat. I bet even Honest Bob would find Uranus a hard planet to sell…

HONEST BOB'S USED PLANETS

"My Bob never tells a single lie – he normally tells lots of them." Bob's mum.

URANUS

What a cute mover – that planet's got style! No, sir, they don't make 'em like this any more! You'll be the envy of all your buddies when you take this planet, with its unique head–over–heels motion, for a roll!

ENJOY LONG, HOT SUMMERS!

If you're sitting at its south pole, you get 42 Earth years of summer when the Sun never sets – followed by 42 years of winter. Oh, dang! I wasn't going to mention the winter! Anyway, it's yours for £11,000,000,000.12 and it's a steal – even if I say so myself!

Hmm, Uranus sounds kinda fun! Let's get back to our sci-fi space story as the aliens whizz towards the planet… What will Oddblob make of oddball Uranus?

Oddblob's Alien Adventure

We were nearing the end of our tour of the Solar System and I wasn't going to be sad to see the Snotties go. I wondered how I'd ever clean that sticky green slime out of my spacecraft!

The next planet we were going to visit was Uranus, but it was just going to be a fly-by. Cosmo had the details – and landing was a bad idea…

BLURBI-DATA

- ☉ **NAME:** Uranus
- ☉ **SIZE:** 52,000 km across
- ☉ **SIZE COMPARED TO EARTH:** 63 times larger
- ☉ **GRAVITY COMPARED TO EARTH:** A bit less
- ☉ **MOONS:** Five main moons and at least 15 smaller ones
- ☉ **LENGTH OF DAY:** 17 Earth hours and 12 Earth minutes
- ☉ **LENGTH OF YEAR:** 84 Earth years
- ☉ **ATMOSPHERE:** Hydrogen and a bit of helium. Methane in the upper clouds gives the planet a greenish look.
- ☉ **WEATHER FORECAST:** It's going to be a bit blowy. But the winds are only 300 km per hour. It's a gentle breeze compared to Saturn.
- ☉ **TRAVEL TIPS:** There's nowhere solid to land. So let's not try.

To be honest, I didn't like Uranus. Its colour reminded me of a spacesick Snotty. The moons looked as boring as an unwanted Blurbi-mas present. I showed the Snotties the best bits – and it didn't take long…

• Uranus has rings like Saturn. But they're only 1.6 km thick and made of black rocks, so they're hard to spot.

• One of the moons – Miranda – has grooves that look like racetracks. That's groovy – snirk, snirk. One of these is called the chevron! Miranda was probably smashed apart by an asteroid and pulled itself back together by gravity.

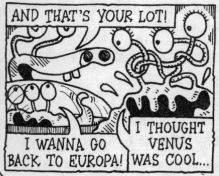 

Bet you never knew!

1 Some of the moons of Uranus are named after characters in plays by William Shakespeare. For example, Titania and Oberon are from A Midsummer's Night Dream. *There's also a character in the play called Bottom, but scientists seem to have "backed out" of naming a moon after him!*

2 Another moon goes by the name of Puck. On Puck you'll find craters called Lob, Butz and Bogle. And no, I didn't make up those names!

How to find a planet in about 23 easy stages

Now, here's a quick question to bamboozle your brain. How many astronomers does it take to discover a planet?

Well, in the case of Neptune, the answer is "quite a few"… But that's not too surprising because, from Earth, Neptune looks like just another star. It's as hard to spot as a needle in a … pin factory.

After a long search, Neptune was eventually tracked down by young scientists, John Couch Adams (1819–1892) and Urbain Le Verrier (1811–1877). We've put them in two rooms, so they can tell their stories separately. These stories begin in 1841, when no one knew that Neptune existed…

111

	ADAMS' STORY	LE VERRIER'S STORY
1845	I've worked out where the new planet is! I'll ask astronomer, George Airy, to find it for me.	I reckon there's a planet beyond Uranus and I know where it is. I've written about it in a scientific journal. I'll ask top astronomers in Paris to find it for me.
1846	Grr — he's not looking! I've called round to see Airy three times but he's never at home.	Grrr — they're not looking for the planet either so I'm sending my ideas to some astronomer pals in Berlin, Germany.
LATER IN 1846	Airy's read my ideas at last and he's asked ace astronomer James Challis to look for the new planet. But so far, nothing. I'm going to miss out on the glory!	Hurrah! The Germans have found the new planet. It's just where I said it was. I'M GOING TO GET THE GLORY!!! CHEERS!

So who actually discovered Neptune? Was it…?

a) Adams. He was the first person to suggest where the planet was.

b) Le Verrier. He made sure the planet was spotted. And in science the credit for a discovery goes to the first person to write about it in a scientific journal – which was Le Verrier.

or **c)** German astronomers Johann Galle and Heinrich d'Arrest. They were the first to find Neptune.

Well, Luke?

Most astronomers would say Adams *and* Le Verrier. But some people would say the answer's **d)** Galileo! The incredible Italian spotted Neptune through his telescope long before anyone else, but he thought it was a star rather than a planet.

Anyway, you'll be pleased to know that when Adams and Le Verrier actually met they became friends, despite not speaking each other's language. (Hmm – Le Verrier was said to have been the rudest man in France, so it may have helped that Adams didn't know what he was saying…)

HELLO, ENGLISH TWIT WHO IS TRYING TO STEAL MY GLORY!*

SHAKE!

HOW TERRIBLY NICE TO MEET YOU!

*WE'VE TRANSLATED HIS FRENCH INTO ENGLISH

Now, you might think that discovering Neptune sounded a tricky business. But the details of the discovery were even more mixed-up than I've made out so far. It's almost as if Neptune *didn't want to be found*!

YEAH — LEAVE ME ALONE!

Before Adams, lots of people thought there was a planet beyond Uranus, but none of them found time to look for it.

COULDN'T BE BOTHERED, MORE LIKE!

James Challis did see Neptune but he thought it was a star. On the evening that he would have got his best view of the planet, he was drinking tea with a friend.

HA, HA! YOU MISSED YOUR CHANCE, MATE!

The boss of the Berlin Observatory, Johann Encke (1791–1865), also missed out on seeing the planet because he was at a party.

"SPACED OUT" ON CHAMPAGNE, I EXPECT!

And now back to our space story. Will the aliens have trouble finding Neptune?

Oddblob's Alien Adventure

With the aid of Cosmo's hyper-speed multi-dimensional navigation systems, I had no difficulties in finding Neptune. The planet looked like Uranus. In fact, it looked enough like Uranus to fool the Snotties…

I pointed out that Neptune's methane clouds are easier to see. Pah! – any alien can spot the difference! I asked Cosmo for the facts. And I made sure the Snotties paid attention.

BLURBI-DATA

- **NAME:** Neptune
- **SIZE:** 48,000 km across
- **SIZE COMPARED TO EARTH:** 58 times larger
- **GRAVITY COMPARED TO EARTH:** A bit stronger than Earth – and Uranus
- **MOONS:** Eight, but at 2,705 km across, Triton is the only large one

🌑 **LENGTH OF DAY:** 16 Earth hours and 6 Earth minutes

🌑 **LENGTH OF YEAR:** 165 Earth years

🌑 **ATMOSPHERE:** Mostly hydrogen, some helium and a smidgen of methane

🌑 **WEATHER FORECAST:** EXTRA EXTREME WEATHER WARNING! It's going to be more stormy than Saturn! Expect winds of 2,000 km an hour – so put that kite away, Oddblob! There'll be methane-snow high in the atmosphere, but it'll melt before it lands.

🌑 **TRAVEL TIPS:** If you dare go near Neptune, Oddblob, I'll erase all your computer games!

Once more we hovered at a safe distance while I pointed out the tourist attractions...

• Neptune has four rings (they're dark and hard to see).
• There's a storm the size of Earth called the Great Dark Spot that travels round the planet backwards.
• There's a cloud called the Scooter that blows around the planet faster than the Spot.

• Triton is the only moon in the Solar System that orbits in the opposite direction to its planet's spin. The pink south pole is made of frozen nitrogen and the rest of the moon is covered in ice.

When the Snotties heard about Triton's ice, they wanted to go there. They enjoyed skating on Europa so much that they wanted to skate on Triton. But Cosmo warned us that Triton is −235°C. It's the coldest place in the Solar System and it could be too cold to visit safely. But did the Snotties listen?

As it happened, the Snotties had great fun skating on the frozen moon. And, for once, there were no problems… Until it was time to leave…

As luck would have it, the spacecraft was parked on a nitrogen geyser. This is a hole where liquid nitrogen blasts from the ground. It's like a hot-water geyser on Earth. The blasting nitrogen turned to gas – it was enough to throw us into space and get our engines going.

And so we set off to Pluto …

The first thing to say about Pluto is that it's *really* far away – on average, 5,193 MILLION km. No wonder the US astronomer who found it, Clyde Tombaugh (1906–1997), had to check 45 million stars over 13 years to see which one moved like a planet. I bet he got a stiff neck.

SPOT THE DISCOVERER OF PLUTO

An interesting idea for younger readers

Mind you, there's one thing harder than finding a new planet – and that's thinking up a name for it! Imagine you had to think up names for places near you. Perhaps you'd name them after your friends…

You could name a putrid-smelling pond after your brother or sister. And you could name a dismal dump after your teacher (or is that a rubbish idea?).

But someone's sure to challenge your choice of names…

Things were much the same with the new planet Clyde Tombaugh found…

Remember Percival Lowell from page 84? Percy died before he found Pluto, but his wife wanted the planet to be named Lowell after him. (I suppose it's better than Planet Percy.) Then she decided it ought to be called Constance after herself.

Percy's astronomer pals hated Constance's idea. The other planets had been named after ancient Roman gods like Mars and Jupiter. The *New York Times* newspaper came up with the name Minerva after the goddess of wisdom.

LIKE THE NEW PLANET, I'M BEAUTIFUL AND MYSTERIOUS...

IT'S A PITY SHE'S NOT 5,900 MILLION KM AWAY!

← ANGRY ASTRONOMERS

Things were just turning nasty when someone in England came up with a better name. Incredibly that someone was just 11 years old. She was a girl named Venetia Burney.

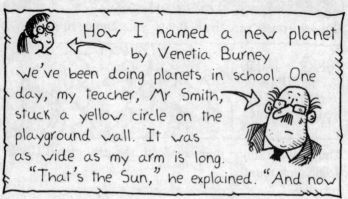

How I named a new planet by Venetia Burney

We've been doing planets in school. One day, my teacher, Mr Smith, stuck a yellow circle on the playground wall. It was as wide as my arm is long.

"That's the Sun," he explained. "And now

we're going for a walk to find out how far away the planets are."

Mr Smith led us across the playground. He was counting out the paces. He walked so fast, his shoes started squeaking. When he reached 30, he bent down and laid a teeny little seed on the ground.

"That's Mercury," he announced, puffing a bit. "Cor - isn't it little?" we said, squinting at the tiny seed.

And that's how I learned that the planets are really small compared to the Sun. And they're a long way apart. The Earth turned out to be a squishy pea on the pavement outside the school. We looked back at the Sun and it looked quite small now. Then my friend Amy trod on the pea by mistake.

"You've just squashed the world!" I said. "Aarggh - a giant foot's just landed on top of us and splatted us flat!"

We headed all the way down the street and across the park until we reached Saturn. There seemed no end to the Solar System. Mr Smith was puffing like a train and his shoes sounded like a couple of noisy mice having a fight. His face was the colour of a sweaty tomato and he was mopping his forehead with a big spotted handkerchief.

"1,019 paces!" gasped Mr Smith. "And this golf ball's Saturn."

We couldn't even see our Sun circle but Mr Smith said that, from the real Saturn, the Sun would just look like a bright star.

"I bet it's cold on Saturn," said Amy with a shiver.

Our teacher was examining his watch. "We'll have to leave it there – Uranus is twice as far from the Sun as Saturn. And Neptune is three times further."

I was glad Mr Smith didn't make us walk to Neptune.

PHEW!

In the afternoon, Mr Smith taught us about the ancient Roman gods. And that's how I knew that the planets were named after gods, but I noticed that some gods didn't have their own planets.

where's my planet?

JUPITER

VENUS

MERCURY

PLUTO

I first heard about the new planet a few weeks later. Mum, Dad, Grandpa and me were having breakfast. As usual, Grandpa was reading the newspaper aloud and, as usual, the news was boring. I was munching my toast loudly so that I wouldn't have to listen. Dad gave me an annoyed look.

"Don't eat so loudly, Venetia," he said.

But just then, Grandpa read something about a new planet and my ears pricked up.

"It's a wonderful discovery," Grandpa was saying. "But astronomers don't know what to call it. The new planet is a very long way from the Sun..."

And that's when I had my great idea.

"I think Pluto would be a good name for it!" I said.

"Don't speak with your mouth full!" said Mum sharply.

I knew Pluto was the Roman god of the underworld and I thought the underworld must be cold and dark like the planet.

But Grandpa was looking at me with interest.

"Well, bless me!" he exclaimed, laying his newspaper on the table. "What a good name for the planet! I must make a note of it. I'll call on my old friend

Mr Turner at the University Observatory and see what he thinks of it."

Mr Turner liked the name so much he sent a special telegram to Mr Tombaugh, the astronomer who found the planet. And all Mr Tombaugh's astronomer friends liked the name so much they decided to use it.

Thinking up planet names is easy! I can't wait for the next planet to be discovered. But there's NO WAY I want to walk there!

Mr Tombaugh

YOU'RE FAR OUT, MAN!

YEAH, IT'S COSMIC, DUDE!

SUN

NEPTUNE'S ORBIT

PLUTO'S ORBIT

Meanwhile, out in space, the huge distances are really getting to the Snotties…

Oddblob's Alien Adventure

We spent half the day travelling to Pluto. And, after five minutes, the Snotties were showing signs of boredom.

IT'S BOR-WING!

When, at last, Pluto came in sight, the Snotties weren't impressed.

IS DAT IT?

YOU'VE BROUGHT US SIX THOUSAND MILLION KM TO SEE THAT?

I asked Cosmo for details. The Snotties were right … Pluto was pathetic!

BLURBI-DATA

- **NAME:** Pluto
- **SIZE:** 2,300 km across
- **SIZE COMPARED TO EARTH:** You could fit 160 Plutos inside the Earth with room to spare
- **GRAVITY COMPARED TO EARTH:** Next to nothing
- **MOONS:** One called Charon. This moon takes one Pluto day to go around the planet. If you're on Pluto, the moon is always in the same place in the sky.

- ☺ **LENGTH OF DAY:** Six Earth days and ten Earth hours
- ☺ **LENGTH OF YEAR:** 248 Earth years
- ☺ **ATMOSPHERE:** A bit of methane and nitrogen
- ☺ **WEATHER FORECAST:** It's going to be VERY COLD – for ever! In fact, when the planet is furthest from the Sun, the whole atmosphere freezes and falls to the ground. It's worse than a cold shower on Triton!
- ☺ **TRAVEL TIPS:** Take a spacesuit and plenty of hot drinks.

I could see Slobslime's hearts (all eight of them) weren't set on a visit to Pluto.

A note to younger readers…

So you weren't impressed by Pluto either? Sorry! Well, if Pluto left you a bit cold (geddit?) here's a special scientific dance. It's sure to warm you up and show why Pluto and Charon are always facing each other…

Dare you discover … the Pluto spin?

What you need:

Two people, ideally an adult parent or teacher, and you! (The adult is going to be Pluto and you are going to be Charon.)

Some groovy music.

What you do:

1 Pluto should put both their hands round Charon's hands and hold tight.

2 Put the music on…

3 Start swinging round and round…

Hold your partner by the hands
And start swinging round and round!
ROUND AND ROUND AND ROUND YOU GO
'Cos you're spinning like old Pluto!

You should notice:

Wheee! This is FUN! Charon's swinging around in a bigger circle than Pluto. Pluto's gravity is strong enough to swing Charon in a bigger circle and hold it in position.

Mind you, some astronomers say that Pluto isn't a planet at all. OK, so it's got a moon and a sort-of atmosphere but it's too tiny to count as a planet, they say. And that's a fair comment, because Pluto's one of thousands of grotty rocky icy thingummies floating about in space beyond Neptune. Astronomers call this area the Kuiper-Edgeworth belt.

Bet you never knew!

In 2002, scientists spotted a mini-planet in the Kuiper-Edgeworth belt. It's about half the size of Pluto and it's called Quaoar (Kwah-o-ar) after a god of the Tongva tribe who used to live in what is now Los Angeles. Hmm – isn't that the sound you make when a dentist tells you to open wide?

Well, that's all for now, folks! As far as the Solar System is concerned, you've had your lot. It was great while it lasted but there's not a lot more to see unless you count the Oort Cloud. This is an area of giant balls of ice and rocks that stretches two light years away from the Sun. It's a bit like a huge field of scattered snowballs…

Cruel comets

The Oort cloud sounds fantastically faraway but those snowballs can come a bit closer to home. When this happens we call them "comets". Here's what happens…

1 A distant star gives a comet a nudge with its gravity.

2 The nudge sends the comet whizzing in the direction of the Sun.

3 As the comet nears the Sun, it starts to melt and the solar wind blows a tail millions of kilometres long behind it. As the comet flies away from the Sun, the tail streams in front of it.

Every year Earth whizzes through clouds of melted comet dust and rock. Then, we see free light shows called meteor showers as the dust and rock burns up in our atmosphere. The meteors make tiny whizzy flashes of light high in the night sky. And it's really exciting counting them and trying to guess where the next one will appear. Here are the best times to see them…

You can see the meteors anywhere in the sky and especially in the eastern half.

Of course, these bits of comet are too small to harm Earth. For that we'd need to be smashed by something really big. Something like an asteroid ... but there's not much danger of that! Er – hold on – let's check the sci-fi story. What's happening on Oddblob's spacecraft...?

Oddblob's Alien Adventure

BLURBI-MESSAGE

A HUGE ASTEROID IS HEADING FOR EARTH. THIS COULD BE THE END OF LIFE AS WE KNOW IT!

OH THAT SOUNDS INTERESTING...

OOPS – I spoke too soon! You'd better turn the page now ... otherwise you'll miss the end of the world!

CAN WE GO AND WATCH, MUM?

THE END-OF-THE-WORLD MOVIE SHOW

There's nothing movie makers like more than a nice Earth-shattering disaster. Something with a budget of billions and big bangs and stunning special effects. But what's the true picture? Are we really going to be destroyed from space? And, oh yes, what's going to happen in our sci-fi space story?

Well, you'll be delighted to know that the answers to all these questions are in this chapter … so read on!

The first thing to say is that most movies about the Earth being wiped out from space are rubbish. The science is WRONG with a capital W – they just couldn't happen in real life.

Spot the silly science screen quiz
Here's a selection of movies from Honest Bob's Used DVD store.

1 Which five really could happen and which three sound like silly science and couldn't ever happen in a Pluto year of Sundays?
2 Which of these five movies could come true some time in the next hundred years?

THE PLANETS OF DOOM

Heave in HORROR as the planets line up and their gravity causes earthquakes and storms on Earth! The end of the world is due at 8.08 pm on 5 May 2000 — so you'd better hide under your bed!

INVASION OF THE SLIMY ALIENS

THEY CAME FROM ANOTHER WORLD TO STEAL OUR PIZZAS AND TURN US INTO JELLY BABIES!

c) THE GOBBLING GALAXY

ARGH!

HELP!

YIKES!

EEK!

Gasp in horror as a giant galaxy gobbles our Milky Way and Earth is hurled into a black hole! It's a hole lot of horror!

THE SPLATTERING STAR d)

WE'RE GONNA DIE LAUGHING!!!

IT'S A QUIET DAY ON EARTH... Suddenly a star blows up and blasts Earth with radiation that turns our atmosphere into laughing gas!

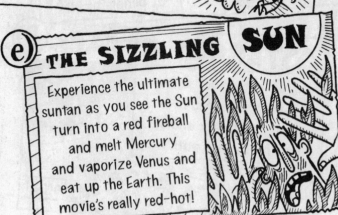

e) THE SIZZLING SUN

Experience the ultimate suntan as you see the Sun turn into a red fireball and melt Mercury and vaporize Venus and eat up the Earth. This movie's really red-hot!

133

f) "THE" "SMASHING" "METEOR" "SHOWER"

Tremble in terror as millions of people get hit on the head by stunning space rocks!

g) THE CRUSHING COMET CRASH

Shudder and shriek as a huge comet crashes into Earth and blasts billions of people to bits.

h) ASTEROID ATTACK

Shout with shock as the Earth is smashed by a giant space rock and all life is wiped out!

OOER!

Now, I bet you want to know why some of the movies are possible and why some of them are as likely as a vegetarian vampire bat … Well, with Luke's help, I've got the answers. Let's start with the movies that just couldn't happen.

Three ways the Earth WON'T get wiped out…

1 The planets lining up

In 2000, the planets appeared close together as seen from Earth. Some people were afraid their gravity would pull on the Earth and cause disaster. So, what happened? Not a lot. The effect on us was weaker than the gravity of the Sun and the Moon.

2 Alien invasion

As Luke was quick to remind me, there's no proof that aliens exist. But if they do, how would they get to travel hundreds of light years through space? And if they could, why would they bother to invade us? If they're that smart, they could make everything they want for themselves using chemicals in space.

135

3 Meteor showers

You may be stunned to read that 20,000 tonnes of space rocks fall on Earth every year – they're mostly lumps of smashed-up asteroids. As they whizz though the air, they're called meteors and if they land they're called meteorites. But don't worry – nearly all meteors burn up before they hit the ground. The only creature ever killed by one was a dog in Egypt in 1911.

Four ways the Earth COULD be wiped out (but not for millions of years)

1 Eaten up by a black hole

In this movie, the Milky Way gets eaten by another galaxy, something that really is possible! Galaxies called (and I love this name!) cannibal galaxies actually pull other galaxies in using gravity and swallow them up. In fact, our Milky Way is a cannibal galaxy because it's currently gobbling up a little galaxy called the Sagittarius Dwarf!

As for our chances of being gobbled, there's a big galaxy called the Andromeda galaxy heading our way at 643,600 km per hour. We'll probably join it to make a bigger galaxy. Many galaxies (including the Milky Way) have black holes in their centres and when the big scrunch happens, some stars could be knocked into the black hole of either galaxy. Panicking yet? Well, DON'T… Andromeda's not due to arrive for THREE BILLION years. So there's plenty of time to finish this book and find somewhere to hide!

2 Splattered by a giant star

If a giant star blew up close to us it would be curtains. Radiation from the blast really could turn our air to nitrous oxide or laughing gas. Sounds fun, doesn't it? Trouble is, the radiation would cook us alive and boil the oceans. But don't go racing off in any rockets just yet. There are no stars near to us that are set to blow – so we're safe for hundreds of millions of years.

3 Sizzled by the Sun

The Sun's too small to blow like a giant star, but it's going to get bigger until it cooks Earth. Here's the sizzling story...

As the Sun uses up all its hydrogen gas fuel, the Sun's centre (or core) shrinks.

What's left of the Sun's core squashes together and heats up.

This makes the outer parts of the Sun swell like a balloon.

As the Sun grows, it cools from white-hot to red-hot. But it's still hot enough to bake us like a burned burger. The outer part of the Sun is lost into space and the core shrinks to a small glowing burned-out star called a white dwarf. Panicking yet? Don't – the big blow-out isn't due for another five billion years.

4 Crushed by a comet

Comets are stony snowballs – so living on Earth is a bit like dodging a gang of snowball-chucking bullies. Except that some of the snowballs are more than 5 km across… But most comets miss us by millions of kilometres and we only get hit by a comet every half a billion years or so.

That still leaves one movie that might just possibly come true…

Asteroid Attack!

Earth gets whacked by an asteroid big enough to wipe out humans every hundred million years – so that's not too often. But scientists reckon Earth's been bashed by three million asteroids of all sizes in its life. There are hits big enough to crush cities every hundred years or so. Luckily, they've missed our cities…

Luke Upwards is so impressed with the science in the *Asteroid Attack!* movie that's he's bought it from Honest Bob.

138

Oh well, Luke, at least you can read our space story. Just to remind you, the asteroid is heading for Earth. It's moving at twice the speed of a bullet. And it means business…

Oddblob's Alien Adventure

We tuned into an Earthling TV station to find out what the humans were doing…

AN ASTEROID IS HEADING FOR EARTH!

AT 10 KM WIDE, IT'S BIG ENOUGH TO END LIFE ON EARTH AS WE KNOW IT!

10 KM

IT LOOKS LIKE THE ASTEROID WILL HIT US WITH THE FORCE OF ALL THE WORLD'S BOMBS. DON'T PANIC! IT'S NOT THE END OF THE WORLD. WELL, YES IT IS…

IT'LL LOOK LIKE THIS

AND NOW FOR THE WEATHER FORECAST…

HOT

FOR 1,000 KM ROUND THE BLAST ZONE IT'LL BE VERY HOT. IN FACT IT'LL BE SO HOT THAT HAIR WILL CATCH FIRE AND EYEBALLS WILL MELT… YIKES — I'M OUTTA HERE!

I figured it would be fun to watch the blast from a distance. But the Snotties didn't like my idea.

For some reason, they thought we had to stop the asteroid. I was just about to blast it with my blurbi-laser when Cosmo stopped me...

BLURBI-DATA

ODDBLOB, LEAVE THAT BUTTON ALONE! You'll blow the asteroid to bits but the flying bits of rock will hit Earth and do even more damage. Here are some Earthling scientists' ideas we could try...

1 Set off a bomb NEAR the asteroid to knock it off course.

2 Put a rocket on the asteroid and knock it to one side.

3 Whack it with a giant air-filled pillow (this idea was suggested by a scientist in 2002).

We didn't have bombs or rockets or giant pillows. So I thought we could sit back and enjoy the show. But Slobslime had other ideas...

For the first time in 1,000 Earth years, Slobslime had had an idea. And what's more – it actually worked!

HURRAH – THE ALIENS HAVE SAVED EARTH! They really are space stars! I wonder what will happen when they get home?

Oddblob's Alien Adventure

I returned to a hero's welcome on Planet Blurb. Unfortunately, the Snotties seemed to be bigger heroes than me.

We were invited to a grand party … but at least I didn't make a fool of myself!

THE END

EPILOGUE
THE SKY'S
THE LIMIT

And so we return to our own blue shiny Earth. OK, so I know it's a bit wet – but as far as the Solar System goes, there really is no place like home. After all, it's the only planet we humans can live on... And now you've seen what the others have to offer, maybe it's the only planet you'd *want* to live on!

Younger readers may think that space reminds them of their worst teacher. It's big and dangerous and it goes on and on for ever. But space is also beautiful and brain boggling. And, best of all, there's much, much more to find out. This book started with a movie and it ended with a story. But the *real-life* adventure of space is just beginning. In the future, there are sure to be millions of...

• New planets to explore.
• New stars to study.
• And perhaps even new friends to meet...?

THANKS FOR SAVING US!